Listen to Us: The World's Working Children

Jane Springer

A Groundwood Book

Douglas & McIntyre

Toronto Vancouver Buffalo

Photo Credits

Page 1: UNICEF/HQ96-0481/Alejandro Balaguer. Page 3: UNICEF/HQ93-2134/Shehzad Noorani. Pages 6, 7 and 8: Reebok International. Page 9: Toronto *Star*/Patti Gower. Page 10: UNICEF/HQ96-0496/Alejandro Balaguer. Page 11: UNICEF/93-1255/Shehzad Noorani. Page 12: UNICEF/HQ93-2132/Shehzad Noorani. Page 13: UNICEF/93-1528/Shehzad Noorani. Page 14(top): Purnima Rao. Page 14 (bottom): Dan Bosler/Tony Stone Images. Page 15 (top): UNICEF/93-18261/Cindy Andrew. Page 15 (center left): UNICEF/93-BOU0031/Maggie Murray-Lee. Page 15 (center right): Mitch York/Tony Stone Images. Page 15 (bottom): UNICEF/5868/Vilas. Page 16: UNICEF/HQ96-0441/José Hernández-Claire. Pages 17 (top): UNICEF/92-122/J. Horner. Page 17 (bottom): UNICEF/93-1257/Shehzad Noorani. Page 18: Rosalyn Train. Pages 19 and 20: UNICEF Nepal. Page 21: Jeff Speed. Page 23: UNICEF/93-1262/Shehzad Noorani. Page 24: Jim West/*Steel Labour*. Page 25 (top): UNICEF/DO194-1254/Mozambique/Giacomo Pirozzi. Page 25 (bottom): UNICEF/Cindy Andrew. Page 27: Jeff Speed. Page 28 (top): UNICEF/5630/Sean Sprague. Page 28 (bottom): UNICEF/1457/Claudio Edinger. Page 30 (top): UNICEF/DO194-1246/Mozambique/Giacomo Pirozzi. Page 30 (bottom left): UNICEF/HQ93-1843/Mozambique/Cindy Andrew. Page 30 (bottom right): UNICEF/89-090/Mozambique/John Isaac. Page 31 (top): UNICEF/HQ96-0453/José Hernández-Claire. Page 31 (middle): UNICEF/HQ96-0440/José Hernández-Claire. Page 31 (bottom): UNICEF/HQ96-0450/José Hernández-Claire. Page 32 (top): UNICEF Nepal. Page 32 (bottom): Jeff Speed. Page 34: UNICEF Nepal. Page 35: UNICEF/HQ96-0641/Gilles Vauclair. Page 37: Child Labor Coalition. Page 38: UNICEF/93-1803/Cindy Andrew. Page 39: UNICEF/5037/Roger LeMoyne. Page 40: UNICEF/5895/Roger LeMoyne. Page 42 (top): UNICEF Nepal/Mani Lama. Page 42 (bottom): Lynn Murray. Page 43: UNICEF/90-262/John Chiasson. Page 44: Jane Springer. Page 45: UNICEF Nepal/Mani Lama. Page 46: UNICEF Nepal/Mani Lama. Page 47 (top): UNICEF/1445/Claudio Edinger. Page 47 (bottom): UNICEF/HQ96-0489/Alejandro Balaguer. Page 48: Jeff Speed. Page 49: UNICEF/HQ96-0234/Nicole Toutounji. Page 50: Derek Lamb and Kai Pindal/Street Kids International. Page 51 (top left and top right): Jeff Speed. Page 51 (bottom right): UNICEF/1443/Claudio Edinger. Page 51 (boxed left): Derek Lamb and Kai Pindal/Street Kids International. Page 53 (top): Toronto *Star*/Andrew Stawicki. Page 53 (bottom): Derek Lamb and Kai Pindal/Street Kids International. Pages 54-55: Toronto *Star*/Andrew Stawicki. Page 56: Jeff Speed. Page 57: Larry Lyons. Page 58: Maureen Hynes. Page 59: UNICEF/HQ96-0089/Giacomo Pirozzi. Page 60: UNICEF/4761/John Chiasson. Page 61: UNICEF/95-0488/Ruth Ansah Ayisi. Pages 62, 64 and 65: Jeff Speed. Page 66: Jane Springer. Page 68 (top): UNICEF/DOI93-1857/Cindy Andrew. Page 68 (bottom): UNICEF/5530/John Isaac. Page 69 (all): Jeff Speed. Page 70: UNICEF/95-0162/Ruth Ansah Ayisi. Pages 72 and 73: Lewis Hine/NCL Committee/Photocollect Gallery, New York. Pages 75 and 76: UNICEF Nepal/Mani Lama. Page 77: UNICEF/HQ96-0497/Alejandro Balaguer. Page 79: UNICEF Nepal/Mani Lama. Page 80 (top): UNICEF/93-1967/Giacomo Pirozzi. Page 80 (left): UNICEF/93-1992/Giacomo Pirozzi. Page 81 (top): UNICEF/5894/Roger LeMoyne. Page 81 (bottom): UNICEF/93-1740/Roger Lemoyne. Page 82: UNICEF/95-1182/Giacomo Pirozzi. Page 84: UNICEF/HQ95-0933/Andrew Beswick. Page 85: UNICEF/5891/Roger LeMoyne. Page 86: UNICEF/HQ96-0737/Shehzad Noorani. Page 87: UNICEF/HQ89-0052/Gilles Vauclair. Pages 89 and 90: Jeff Speed. Page 91: Toronto *Star*/Anne Munro. Page 93: UNICEF/HQ96-0724/Shehzad Noorani.

Copyright © 1997 by Jane Springer

All rights reserved. No part of this book may be reproduced, stored in a retrieval system or transmitted in any form, or by any means, without the prior written permission of the publisher or, in the case of photocopying or other reprographic copying, a licence from CANCOPY (Canadian Reprography Collective), Toronto, Ontario.

Groundwood Books / Douglas & McIntyre Ltd.
585 Bloor Street West, Toronto, Ontario M6G 1K5

Distributed in the U.S.A. by
Publishers Group West
4065 Hollis Street, Emeryville, CA 94608

We acknowledge the support of the Canada Council for the Arts and the Ontario Arts Council for our publishing program.

Book design by Michael Solomon
Printed and bound in China by
Everbest Printing Co., Ltd.

Photographs, page 1: A boy carries a pumice stone quarried from an underground volcanic mine near Arequipa in southern Peru; page 3: girls working on a construction site in Bangladesh.

Library of Congress data is available.

Canadian Cataloguing in Publication Data
Springer, Jane
    Listen to us: the world's working children
"A Groundwood book".
Includes bibliographical references and index.
ISBN 0-88899-291-2 (bound)
ISBN 0-88899-307-2 (pbk.)
1. Children - Employment - Juvenile literature.
I. Title.
HD6231.S67 1997   j331.3'1   C97-931626-X

For Peg and John

Contents

doing repetitive, unskilled labor, not learning a skilled craft.

Most kids in North America and Europe today do chores around the home. They make meals, wash dishes, take out the garbage (or give their parents lessons in how to use the Internet!). This work is usually unpaid, but many kids get an "allowance" to pay for some of their school or entertainment expenses. Others are paid for odd jobs they do outside their homes, like babysitting. Some deliver papers or work in fast-food restaurants. Some have left home and now live on the streets, making a living any way they can.

Is any of this child labor? Or is it work that prepares children for life—work that is useful for oneself or others? It depends on a number of factors. Do the children or teenagers have any choice about the work they do? How many hours do they work? How much are they being paid? Do they go to school? Is the work dangerous to their physical or mental health? Are they any better off for doing the work? What, if anything, are they learning from their work? Who is benefiting from the work—the child, the parent, or just the employer?

Some experts have outlined three basic types of child labor. There are children who work with their families—on the farm, in the home or for a family business. Second, there are those who are paid to work in factories or who have been hired out or even sold by their families to do farm work, domestic work or to work as soldiers. Then there are those who have been thrown out of their homes by their parents, or who have run away and who will do any kind of work in order to survive—street children.

In general, the worst and most exploitative types of child labor are found where children are working in profit-seeking enterprises outside their homes. But children who work at home may be exploited as well. Families are not always the safe places we would hope they are. Children who do work that is too hard, that takes too much time or is harmful to their health are being exploited—whether they are doing housework or factory work.

The International Labor Organization (ILO) estimates that there are 250 million children between the ages of five and fourteen working in developing countries. One-half of them work full time. One-third of them work in extremely dangerous conditions. If the large numbers of exploited children (mainly girls) who work with their families, plus all street children were added, the total would swell by several hundred million.

Suresh, a street kid, roasts peanuts all day to earn about fifty cents. He is working under the bridge where he lives in Kathmandu, Nepal.

Children work in many different ways.

In the capitalist or "free market" system, people agree to work for someone else in return for pay. They are exchanging their work for wages. There is often a struggle between workers and employers over how much the work is worth. Many employers want to pay their workers as little as legally possible because the less money they pay the workers, the more they will have left over as profit.

If you are giving a lot more in work than you're getting back in terms of money or other rewards, you are being exploited. That means that someone else is profiting from your labor—selling their product for more than it costs them to produce it.

Multinational fast-food chains, for example, make enormous profits. One way they manage to do this is by employing mainly young people and some old people (one group that has not yet really entered the labor market and another that has already left it). Both groups can be paid less than regular adult workers. Both accept irregular hours, unpaid breaks and a lack of benefits. Both are being exploited.

Being oppressed is worse than not being given an equal exchange for your work. Oppression includes control by force (or the threat of force). Oppression is an abuse of human rights. However exploitative working for a fast-food hamburger chain might be, it is only oppressive if someone forces you to work there, or abuses you physically or emotionally on the job. Forced or bonded labor is a form of oppression. Adults misusing their power over children is also a form of oppression.

A young girl works in the noonday sun in a tobacco field in Mexico.

Poverty

Children work in exploitative situations for many reasons. The first and most obvious is because their families are poor and need their income to survive. Most children who live in poverty in the industrialized countries are protected from out-and-out starvation by social welfare systems. In developing countries, however, families often have only themselves to depend on. While even a "poor" child in Canada or the U.S. eats three meals a day, has a home to live in and goes to school, millions of children in developing countries are malnourished, homeless and never attend school. They are unprotected if their parents are unemployed or ill, if the weather destroys their crops or if their house (if they're lucky enough to have one) burns down. In situations like this, everyone in the family helps out.

Hundreds of millions of children work because they are poor. But child labor would not be so common or so harmful unless there were people who were willing to exploit poor children and their families. The poorer the children and the more desperate their situation, the easier it is for an employer to exploit them.

Above: Street kids asleep in Brazil.

Left: Girls and women load bricks under the watchful eye of their boss in Nepal.

Minority Groups

Most child workers come from extremely poor families. Most are also members of minority groups. The weaker the position people are in, the more open they are to oppression and exploitation. In India, for example, where Hindus represent 80 percent of the population, the minority Dalits (and other low castes) and Muslims make up a large percentage of child labor.

These attitudes may not be so systematized in the rest of the world, but they are there just the same. The largest proportion of child workers in the United States are Mexican migrants who have few of the rights accorded American citizens. In Vancouver, Canada, aboriginal girls make up a significant proportion of the city's downtown sex workers. In Brazil, the majority of child workers are the children of indigenous peoples or the descendants of African slaves.

Girls

The international women's movement has fought hard to improve women's economic and social status over the last twenty-five years but in most parts of the world, girls are still brought up to be wives and mothers and prepared for a status that is inferior to men. As child workers are inferior to adult workers (and women workers are inferior to men workers), so in most cases girl workers are inferior to boys.

Girls and their mothers do most of the unpaid work in the home. And girls worldwide are often only able to get waged jobs that resemble

Below left: A Dalit girl stacks water buffalo dung patties (to be used as fuel) in India.

Below right: A Calcutta street girl and her little brother welcome a banana in exchange for a photo.

THE CASTE SYSTEM

For thousands of years of in India, Hindu tradition has said that only certain people are fit to do certain types of work. According to Hindu creation mythology, the highest-caste Brahmans are "born" to be poets or priests. Next come the Kshatriyas who are warriors and kings, then the Vaishyas, who are merchants and landowners, and at the bottom are the Shudras, the landless laborers.

The caste system has gone through many changes over two thousand years, and it was made illegal by the government of India in 1950. Yet its effects are still felt today, especially

in the rural areas of the country. Many descendants of the Shudras—the "Untouchables" or Dalits—are still expected to do the dirtiest and the most dangerous jobs.

Girls in Nepal work for their families or in a quarry, breaking rocks into gravel for use in construction.

that work: cleaning, cooking, laundry, caring for children, serving food and drinks. They work as domestics, as nannies, as cleaners or waitresses in hotels, restaurants and bars. Sex work is also linked to their traditional role as an object for men's pleasure. In waged work, as well as at home, they are expected to put the well-being of others above their personal needs.

But girls also work in many of the same areas as boys: carpet weaving, making clothing, crafts and toys. There are twice as many girls as boys working in quarries (where building stones are extracted and cut or broken) and factories in India, and most of the children who work in construction are girls.

An extreme example of the subservient situation of girls is the case of Nepal, a small mountainous country that borders on India. There, as a 1991 Child Workers in Nepal publication notes, "the birth of a girl is usually marked with sorrow as if some great misfortune had befallen her parents and family."

Parents make very clear that they want sons, not daughters. Why? Because sons acquire property and the family name. Daughters must be provided with a dowry when they marry. (A dowry is the money or goods that in some communities a bride's family pays the groom's family at the time of marriage.)

Once she is married, a daughter leaves to live with her husband's family. She is considered to be of no use to her own family any longer. In fact, she is a burden. As a result, girl babies are fed less than boys and are less likely to be taken to a health center if they are sick. Girls start work sooner, are made to work harder and are much less likely to go to school than their brothers. Nepali girls are married off very young—almost half before they are sixteen—and they are expected to have children right away. The only identity they have is in relation to the men in their family.

Women have some advantages over men. They live longer. Nepal is the only country in the world where women's life expectancy (52) is lower than men's (56).

Globalization

As we approach the end of the twentieth century a number of trends together have helped to make child labor more widespread than ever.

Growing industrialization has made large companies bigger and more powerful. They have greater influence on government policies than in the past. These companies are continually looking for new markets— more people to buy their products or services. They enlarge their markets by putting pressure on governments to develop trade agreements

Children in developing countries spend huge amounts of time collecting firewood and feed for animals.

There are more homeless people in the world than ever before. These people live in Toronto.

like the European Union, the North American Free Trade Association and the proposed Pacific Rim Accord. These agreements allow companies to move their factories to a place or a country where they can produce their goods more cheaply, as well as find people to buy their goods. At the same time, the companies encourage governments to get rid of laws that guarantee a minimum wage and benefits like medical care or a pension plan, and that allow workers to organize themselves to form unions.

The easiest way to produce goods more cheaply (and therefore be more competitive) is to cut back on the price of labor. This means firing workers and/or reducing their wages. It is difficult to lower the wages of adults who are still protected by trade unions (although these days, some unions are accepting wage cuts, thinking it will save their jobs). Hiring children in developing countries to work for little money or bare subsistence (food and a place to sleep) is a solution.

In order to lower costs, large factories that make cars, for example, are reorganized so that only the final assembly is done in the factory. Production of the individual car parts is "outsourced" or "subcontracted." This means the work is given to individuals or smaller firms. The same happens with clothing manufacturers who contract out sewing to small sweatshops. A large number of small shops are harder to regulate than one large one, so these small companies may get away with paying adults the minimum wage or lower, or they may employ children.

In the industrialized world, where child labor laws are more widely enforced, children are not exploited to the same extent. But in unregulated industries, like agriculture, working children enable employers to increase their profits. In the United States, for example, hiring children and their parents saves the agricultural industry an estimated $3 billion a year. And American corporations save $28 billion a year by hiring part-time teenaged workers at lower wages than they would have to pay regular adult workers.

Globalization is the word that describes the whole process of big corporations moving around the world in search of new markets and cheaper labor. It has enormous effects on everybody, but especially on people who are poor. Peasants in developing countries who have been mainly growing their own food to live on lose the little they have as better-off farmers who grow cash crops (e.g., coffee, tea, tobacco, sugar) to export to other countries take over their land. Using land for cash crops also means that fewer basic foods like rice or maize (corn) are grown for local markets, and what is available costs more. Forests are clear-cut for farmland. As trees become more scarce, women and children in developing countries spend more time looking for wood to burn so they can cook their food. As more water is pumped for factories and huge farms, peasants must go farther to fetch water. Overworked rural children become easy prey for exploitative labor contractors who come to their villages to offer a "good deal" in the city.

People who can no longer grow their own food need some income. Women and children especially may have to move into low-paying jobs in the export industries. Or children may have to work at home so their parents can earn wages outside the home. And as people become landless, they first move toward the cities in their own countries looking for work, and then out toward other countries.

With all this pressure to produce for export, governments tend to ignore harmful working conditions and companies that break labor laws. Human rights violations become more common. Governments everywhere are spending less money on health, education and social welfare—areas that have a direct impact on children's lives. Fewer children are able to go to school and fewer poor families are given assistance, which in turn worsens the situation of child labor. Child labor is also affected by countries in Europe and North America accepting fewer immigrants. Poor families have little choice but to send their children out to work.

In today's world, countries are not as sealed off as they were in the past. Instead, the world is economically dominated by the three hundred leading banks and industrial transnationals (companies that operate freely across the borders of a number of different countries). More and more, they are the ones who make the decisions that affect us all.

These companies do not have all the power, however. Modern communications and technology make it easier for people to meet and talk about common concerns—about human rights, including the right of children not to work, about the growing gap between rich and poor, about the destruction of the environment. Child-labor activists, environmentalists, peace activists, indigenous peoples and trade unions recognize that poor people the world over are becoming more excluded from the decision-making that affects their lives. They are organizing on the Internet, at conferences and seminars, by fax and telephone and through the media to assert their rights. And their voices are being heard. Iqbal's message about the plight of bonded child workers in his country could never have reached us without the work of non-governmental organizations in Pakistan and their supporters around the world.

A study of children working in Penang, Malaysia, found that only 13 percent kept their earnings for themselves. These children then paid for their own school fees, food and entertainment. The rest contributed at least half of their income to their families. A Bangladesh study found that 50 percent of 12,000 children working in the garment industry were the sole supporters of their families.

Listen to Us

Employers Like Child Workers

Children cost less and are easier to dominate than adults. Although, as Iqbal Masih has shown, a few children do resist, in general, children are smaller, physically weaker and less experienced than adults, and they do not resist their conditions as forcefully as adults do.

Some employers argue that children are better suited to certain tasks than adults. People who want to justify child labor often use the "nimble fingers" argument. They claim that children are better than adults at detailed work like knotting carpets or stitching clothes or soccer balls because their fingers are smaller and therefore more dextrous. But adults from all cultures have been doing intricate hand-knotting, stitching and embroidery for centuries. It is true that children can be taught to be dextrous at a job. But that does not mean that they are better at it than adults.

Some industries have developed child-sized machines. And some farmers say that children are the best workers for picking certain crops that ripen close to the ground. But in both cases, it is because employers want to use children as cheap labor, not because they have been proven to be best at the work. In fact, much of the work children do is monotonous or menial. One reason they are hired for some jobs is because they can be forced to do work that adults do not want to do.

These girls gather yarn in a carpet factory in Nepal.

The wage rates of children who work in factories in developing countries is about one-quarter to one-third that of adults.

HOW UNIONS PROTECT WORKERS

It is hard for anyone to ask the boss for a raise in pay, or safer equipment or better washroom facilities. It is much easier to ask as part of a group. Workers form unions in order to face their employer collectively. Together, they negotiate a contract with the employer that outlines wages, hours of work and hiring and firing practices. A contract may also detail working conditions, health and safety regulations, benefits (e.g., pension, health care, special bonuses), prohibit child labor and discrimination on the basis of gender (whether you are a man or a woman), ethnic origin and sexual orientation. In most countries, the wages of unionized workers are much higher than those of non-unionized workers, and their jobs are usually more secure. While it would certainly be beneficial for child workers to form unions, it is against the law in most countries. They're too young.

Wal-Mart workers outside their store in Windsor, Canada, the first of more than 2,600 stores worldwide to have a union.

Most of the children who spend their days working live in the developing countries of Asia, Africa and Latin America. Working children are becoming increasingly common in eastern Europe, however, with the breakdown of the former Soviet Union. And though the numbers are much smaller, children also work in the industrialized countries of Europe and North America, in Japan and Australia.

Africa has the highest proportion of children working—40 percent of children between five and fourteen work—although the largest numbers of children work in Asia. Children work in a wide range of occupations, but the largest portion of them, especially in Africa and Latin America, work for their families, either in the home, in the fields or on the street.

It is difficult to get reliable figures on the number of child workers around the world. Employers and governments do not want to advertise the fact that they use child labor, so they don't keep records. People or organizations that try to gather information about working children are often harassed by employers or given the wrong information or prevented from entering sweatshops and factories and brothels to get the facts themselves. When they do go into children's workplaces and interview

4. Where Do We Find Child Labor?

Almost half of all African children work. This Mozambican girl is returning to her home from neighboring Malawi where her parents fled the war.

Where Children Work
Percentage of Working Children by Region

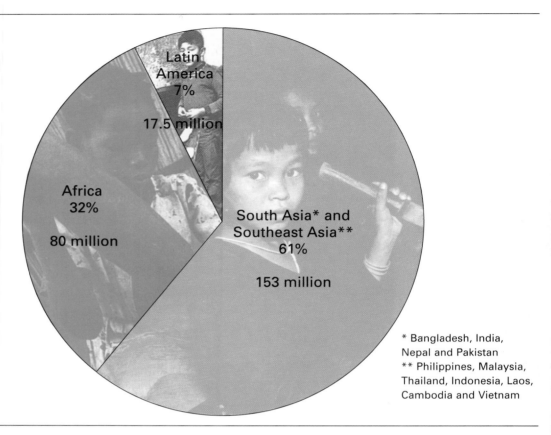

Latin America
7%
17.5 million

Africa
32%
80 million

South Asia* and Southeast Asia**
61%
153 million

* Bangladesh, India, Nepal and Pakistan
** Philippines, Malaysia, Thailand, Indonesia, Laos, Cambodia and Vietnam

children about their jobs, they may be setting them up for a beating from their employers. So it is not easy to get a clear picture of the situation.

However, we do have reliable estimates of the number of children who attend primary school around the world. According to the United Nations Children's Fund (UNICEF), 140 million children between the ages of six and eleven in developing countries—about 90 million of them girls—never enrol in school. They work in their own homes doing domestic labor or on the family farm, or they sell food on the street or work as servants or nannies. Almost as many children drop out of school before they finish—so they may also be working. Add to this the number of child workers who go to school as well as work and therefore appear in official statistics as pupils rather than as workers, and you can see that the ILO's estimate of 250 million working children is almost certainly low. But these huge numbers tell us, at the very least, that the situation cannot be ignored. A group of young people at least as large as the population of the United States is at work worldwide, not just missing out on schooling and an opportunity for a better life, but cutting their lives perilously short.

GIRLS' WORK IS HIDDEN

There are no overall figures to show how many working children are girls and how many are boys. Where there are figures on the numbers of boys and girls in a particular type of work, they usually show that there are fewer girls. However, if the chores that girls do in the home were counted, the percentage of girls who work would double or even triple. It is likely that all of the 90 million girls around the world who are not in school are working—most of them at home.

A servant girl scrubs a sidewalk in New Delhi, India.

Above: A gypsy girl and her baby sister beg in front of a hotel in Prague, capital of the Czech Republic.

Right: A Brazilian boy sifts through garbage to make a living. Neither begging nor ragpicking are included in official statistics of child workers (see chart opposite).

Child Workers and Type of Work* in Selected Countries

Country	Age	Estimated Number of Child Workers	Occupation
Bangladesh	10-14	6-15 million	garments, hotel, fish processing, transport
Brazil	under 14	3.5-7.5 million	charcoal, sugar cane, shoes, oranges, textiles, garments, tin mining
Cambodia	5-17	600,000	agriculture, sex work
Canada	under 16	8,000	agriculture, garments, sex work
China	+	+	textiles, garments, fireworks, toys, footwear, electronics, road construction, agriculture
Colombia	12-17	1 million	cut flowers, coffee, leather, coal and emerald mining
Côte d'Ivoire	+	+	gold and diamond mining, fish canning, sugar cane
Egypt	6-14	1.5 million	cotton, carpets, perfume, leather
Guatemala	7-14	1 million	sugar cane, coffee, garments
Haiti	under 14	250,000	domestics
India	under 14	44-100 million	carpets, gemstones, brassware, glassware, shoes, silk, matches, fireworks, many others
Indonesia	10-14	2.7 million	garments, wood, furniture
Italy	8-14	+	leather
Lesotho	12-15	+	textiles, garments, milling, canning, leather, jute, handicrafts
Mexico	under 15	8-11 million	factories, sweatshops, farms, on the street
Morocco	under 15	10,000	carpets, garments, leather
Nepal	under 14	3 million	agriculture, carpets, garments, handicrafts
Pakistan	50% under 10	10-19 million	agriculture, carpets, leather, footwear, mining
Peru	under 15	7.5 million	informal economy, forced labor in gold mines of Madre de Dios
Philippines	under 15	5.6 million	agriculture, food production, fireworks, footwear, furniture, mining
Portugal	under 16	30,000-200,000	footwear, garments, ceramics, granite paving-stone industry
Tanzania	10-14	400,000	sisal (for cord and twine), gemstones, agriculture, fishing
Thailand	7-14	4-5 million	sweatshops, garments, gemstones, leather, shrimp and seafood, furniture, sex work
Turkey	6-14	4 million	domestic labor, agriculture, industry, service
United States	under 16	900,000	agriculture, garments, sex work
Zimbabwe	7-14	240,000	agriculture, chrome and gold mining

* This does not include unpaid work at home or on the farm or most work in the informal sector, because country statistics do not usually include them.
+ Statistics are not available.

5. What Work Do Children Do?

Agricultural Work

Subsistence Agriculture
More children around the world work in agriculture than in any other area. Most work with their own families. In developing countries, where a large part of the population still lives in the rural areas, many people practice subsistence agriculture, meaning they grow the food they need to live on. For this, the labor of everyone in the family is necessary, although women and girls usually do more of the work in the fields than men and boys.

As countries move toward a free market economy (see page 20), few of these farm families can still survive without cash, the way they did in the past. As more men and boys (and some women) are drawn into the waged labor market, the burden of the work at home is left even more on the shoulders of women and girls.

Because "helping out" on the farm has traditionally been seen as a natural and healthy type of work for children, there are no laws against it as there are against other types of child labor. As well, since it has been assumed that you cannot be exploited if you are working with your family, it is not counted in child labor statistics. The fact that children are not paid for it makes farm work seem insignificant. Yet children's work on the farm contributes greatly to a family's survival.

These Mozambican children are all working to help their families produce food.

These children all work on a tobacco plantation in Mexico.

Commercial Agriculture

Other children work in commercial agriculture. They are hired out to employers to do farm work. While they may still work alongside their families, the situation is usually more exploitative because they are working for someone else. This means they are usually far away from their home villages, and they have no control over their hours or working conditions. Commercial farms make extensive use of chemical fertilizers and pesticides so the work is also more likely to be dangerous.

Most farm workers work during the planting and harvest seasons and move around to different areas as their work is needed. The work is full time at certain periods of the year and irregular or non-existent at other times. Children may go to school during the slow work periods, but most are too busy working during the seeding and harvest seasons.

The ILO estimates that around 2 million of the 20 million people employed on the world's plantations are children. Plantations are large farms that produce crops such as tea, sugar cane, rubber, bananas, cocoa (from which chocolate is produced), groundnuts (peanuts), cotton, tobacco and rice.

WHAT IT MEANS TO BE A MIGRANT

Migrant workers leave their home village to work in the city or leave their home country to work in another country. They are cut off from their extended families and communities. If they move to another country, they may not speak the language, may not know what their rights are and, in many cases, are at the mercy of their employers. This is true of Nepali girls kidnapped or duped into working as prostitutes in India. It is true of Mexican children who accompany their parents to work on farms in the U.S. and Canada. It is true of Mozambican children whose lives in their own country have been destroyed by the war that lasted until 1992. Fleeing alone or with members of their families to South Africa, they are hired by local farmers. Often, before paying them, the farmers report them as illegal aliens who must be deported.

Two Mexican boys slip through a fence to cross the border into the United States.

In the Central American countries of Guatemala and Honduras, children as young as six work with their parents on huge coffee plantations. They usually pick and sort beans, but they also carry sacks of coffee that weigh up to 150 pounds. Sometimes they apply fertilizers and pesticides, without any masks or gloves to protect them from the fumes. During the harvesting season, the children work eight to twelve hours a day.

A large portion of the children working in agriculture are bonded laborers. Countries with substantial numbers of bonded child agricultural workers include Nepal, India, Pakistan and Brazil.

In India, there are more bonded child laborers in agriculture than in any other industry or service. They work long hours, seven days a week, usually receive only two meals a day and do very difficult work. Sanjeev, an eleven-year-old interviewed by Human Rights Watch in 1995, works every day of the year, with no time off for illness. He takes care of animals and works in the fields from 5 A.M. until 9 P.M. or 10 P.M. Once a year, his family receives about $75 for his work.

Agricultural Work in North America

There are about 800,000 child farm workers in the United States, many of them migrants. Agriculture is the largest area of child work in the U.S. Why? Because, as everywhere else in the world, farm work has been seen as healthy because it is out of doors and because it trains the children of peasants and farmers to become farmers themselves. While most countries have laws to regulate children's work in industry, farm work is usually not included. When it was enacted in 1935, the U.S. National Labor Relations Act did not allow farm workers to organize to form a union. As a result, employer farmers still get away with wages or piece rates (a fixed price per "piece" or bucket or bushel) that work out to rates far below the minimum wage, as well as poor working and living conditions. They also get away more easily with using child labor than do employers in any other industry. In fact, the only way adult farm workers can make enough money to support their families is with the help of their children, whose work increases their own piece-work wages.

Farm work is seasonal. Migrant workers must travel huge distances to harvest the various crops as they ripen. They are often cheated by employers or contractors. Farm-worker families make only one-quarter of the U.S. national average income. The work is tedious. Worse, it is dangerous. Children's bodies are more vulnerable to being poisoned from pesticides because children are shorter and work closer to the

Bonded labor is a system in which a poor family exchanges the labor of one of its members—often a child—for a small fee or "loan." In South Asia, especially in India, Pakistan and Nepal, millions of children are handed over to work as farm or factory workers. Bonded labor is also practiced in Thailand, Sri Lanka, Kuwait, Bolivia, Colombia, Brazil, the Dominican Republic and parts of West Africa.

The bondage involves whole families in some cases, and the "debt" can be inherited. This means that a small child may be working to pay off a debt contracted by her father or even her grandfather. The amount of money owed is usually very small—$35 is the average amount "lent" for bonded children in India. But it is a lot for poor people who cannot get a loan any other way and do not have the kind of social assistance available in most industrialized countries.

Bonded labor is really a form of slavery, except that an amount of money is initially paid to the family. The family may think the situation is temporary, but it almost never is, because there is no chance to pay off the debt. If they or their families were fairly paid for the work they do, it would not take long to work off the debt. But in most cases, the children are paid extremely little or are not paid at all. In addition, they are often told they can only cancel the debt by paying it all at once. This is impossible under their conditions.

The situation of bonded laborers is as grim as that of slaves. The employer/master has control over the child twenty-

four hours a day, and physical and sexual abuse are common. Most bonded laborers do not get enough to eat, and living conditions are bad. One twelve-year-old Pakistani carpet weaver said, "My master bought, sold and traded us like livestock."

It is hard to believe that such situations really exist. How can parents be so poor that they would "sell" their child? How do employers get away with "buying" a child from his parents, putting him to work many hours a day, scarcely feeding him, mistreating him and never paying him? The explanation is not simple, but in India, for example, it involves a series of power relationships. Although it is illegal, the caste system still operates in much of rural India (see page 18). Most owners of large farms are from the high caste, small landown-

It is estimated that 15 million children work as bonded laborers in India. Only 5 percent of them can read. Most of them work in agriculture (between 52 and 87 percent). Others work in the beedi (cigarette) industry (right), in the carpet-weaving (left) and silk-weaving industries. Bonded children also work making silver jewelry, leather shoes and cutting and polishing gems.

ers are from a lower caste, and those who have no land and bonded laborers are at the bottom. Low-caste adults, most of them illiterate, find it difficult to negotiate a decent bargain with the wealthy high-caste adults who become the child's master/employer. The employers are often linked by family or caste to local police and administrators, so it is useless to try to enlist the help of the law.

ground. As well, their nervous and reproductive systems are still developing. (Studies have linked pesticide exposure to brain tumors and leukemia.) Children also have more accidents than adults because they are weaker and cannot tolerate the exposure to weather and the repetition of field work. They regularly suffer from back and wrist strains. In the U.S., three hundred children a year die in farm machinery and tractor accidents. The lack of good water and sanitation at their work sites also means that many workers get parasitic infections (diarrhea). Many don't get enough to eat. Forty-five percent of migrant agricultural child laborers drop out of school, which is three times the national average. The life expectancy of U.S. farm workers is only forty-nine, compared to seventy-three for the general U.S. population.

The United Farm Workers of America, founded by the late Cesar Chavez, himself a former child migrant worker, is struggling to organize Californian farm workers to change these conditions and stop children from working in the fields.

In Canada, the situation is not as severe as in the U.S., and it is difficult to get figures on the numbers of child farm workers. However, Zindabad, the Canadian Farm Workers' Union formed in British Columbia in 1980, reports that almost a quarter of the 28,000 workers bring their children with them into the fields because they have no one to take care of them. Clearly, a large percentage of these children are working alongside their parents.

The other main area where migrant farm workers are used is in southern Ontario. In the summer, Mexican migrant laborers, chiefly Mennonite families, may start work at 7 A.M. and not finish until 7 P.M. Sara Peters, fourteen, described the work to CTV reporter Peter Murphy as "hot, tiring and *boring.*" Their employer said it was common to have whole families working during the summer months, but that it was "discouraged" during the school year, when an "exemption" was needed to allow the children to work. In other words, it is not difficult to get around the laws restricting the use of child labor in agriculture, even in the industrialized world.

Susana

Susana, Age 17, United States, Farm Worker

Susana Vasquez was born in Mexico and migrated with her family to the U.S. when she was seven. By the time she was nine, she was working with her parents in the fields of Pennsylvania, picking fruit and vegetables. She dug potatoes, picked apples, peaches, cucumbers and green peppers. She worked on hot dry days when there was no water available except costly bottled water. She worked on cold rainy days when the fields were muddy. During one season, she worked after school from 4 P.M. to 8:30 P.M. picking twenty huge buckets of tomatoes. On the weekends she picked sixty buckets between 7 A.M. and 7 P.M. She was paid $1 a bucket, which the grower then sold for $12 each. Susana also picked strawberries. "I liked picking the strawberries because I could eat them if I was hungry," she says.

At every new place and new job, Susana translated for her father as he negotiated with the farmer over work, pay and living arrangements. Like other migrant farm workers, Susana's family often stayed in camps with poor cooking and food storage facilities. There was often no access to drinking water or toilets in the fields. "Talking about all those things scared me," she remembers. However, she admits that she is stronger and more mature as a result than the other kids she knows.

"There was no time for going to movies or to do homework. I often fell asleep in class," Susana says. She changed school three times a year as her family traveled to find work, and her grades were low. "Just as I adjusted, it was time to move again."

Susana is now seventeen and in grade ten in Salisbury, Maryland. She has been held back two grades because of the many interruptions in her studies. "How I wish my parents could have gotten other jobs," she says. "It isn't easy for me, but it's certainly not easy for them either.... Next time you buy a tomato, think of me as a nine-year-old."

Domestic Work

Domestic Work in the Home

The work we do in our own homes is called domestic labor. It includes growing, harvesting, buying, preparing and serving food, child care, caring for the sick and elderly, laundry and housecleaning. It is unpaid and, everywhere in the world, it is done mainly by women and girls. (If someone from outside the home is paid to do this work, the worker is called a domestic, maid or servant.)

In the developing world, the fact that children do much of this work enables many households to survive. The father or mother may earn a

Two girls pound maize in Mozambique.

small wage selling vegetables or working in a cottage industry. Meanwhile, children tend the fields, care for their younger siblings and cook and clean. The children's work allows the people who employ their parents to save on labor costs because they're not providing all the money (or food) that the family needs to live.

Researchers know even less about children's domestic labor than they do about the other work that children do. This is in part because it is "just housework," an ordinary fact of life in every household. It is also less rigidly planned and controlled than paid work, and no real product is produced at the end of it. In fact, it must be done again and again, as long as there are family members to be fed and cared for and a house to be cleaned. Finally, it is given less value because it is done by women and girls.

Girls begin work in their homes at an earlier age than their brothers and work about seven hours more a week. In many developing countries, little girls begin to care for a younger brother or sister at the age of three or four and often help with other chores like carrying water or preparing food.

A Nigerian mother told UNICEF that it made no sense to send her daughter to school because, "Who then is going to look after the babies, fetch water, clean and cook when I go to market to sell my vegetables? Who is going to help me dig, weed and harvest?"

The boys don't do it. Boys are given a lighter load and more often are encouraged to go to school. One study showed that of thirteen household tasks that girls in developing countries regularly performed, only two—chopping and collecting wood—were also done by boys. And because the girls do more work, a family loses more by sending a

Woineshet Getachew is fourteen, goes to school part time and dreams of becoming a doctor. She lives in Ethiopia.

daughter to school than by sending a son.

As more families worldwide are struggling harder to make enough money to buy food, mothers who used to work at home are now being forced to work for wages or in the informal market (e.g., selling vegetables). The more mothers work outside the home, the more their daughters must work on domestic activities and the less time they have to go to school or to do homework if they do manage to get to school.

Girls do more domestic labor in the industrialized economies as well.

Two girls carry water to their homes in a camp for internal refugees in Cambodia.

While boys may do such jobs as washing the car and garden work, girls tend to do constant daily chores like housekeeping and child care. And girls spend more time each week on the work they do. For example, in Canada in 1992, teenaged girls spent 80 minutes a day on household chores and volunteer work, 30 minutes more per day than teenaged boys.

It is important that children contribute to their households. But any child who works so long and hard that she cannot go to school must be considered to be a child worker. Even in cases where they also manage to go to school, many girls are still forced to work hard in their homes and are expected to take care of their family's needs before their own.

Domestic Work Outside the Home

Millions of girls and boys work as servants in other people's homes. They clean, cook and look after small children. Most are on call twenty-four hours a day. They may sleep with the family baby or children so they can wake up with them and look after them. Otherwise they are likely to sleep on the kitchen floor or in a back hallway. Their food is the family's leftovers and their pay is small. They have no time for school and often no time off to visit their families. They are like prisoners in someone else's household.

There are an estimated 5 million child domestic workers in Indonesia, 500,000 in Sri Lanka, 250,000 in Haiti and 200,000 in Kenya. In Venezuela, 60 percent of working girls between ten and fourteen are employed as domestics. There are unknown numbers of children working as domestics all over Africa, Asia, Latin America, the Middle East and parts of the south of Europe.

In *Small Hands: Children in the Working World,* Rachel Marcus and Caroline Harper note that one of the few organizations working directly with child domestic workers is Foyer Maurice Sixto (FMS), in Haiti. FMS runs centers for children known as restaveks. Along with basic education classes, FMS attempts to develop the children's confidence, which has been badly affected by their work. They also put pressure on the employers to provide better working conditions.

Top: A Nepali metal worker tries to protect his eyes with dark glasses.

Bottom: Boys in a bakery in Peru.

Industrial Work

Children work in hundreds of small industries around the world. These include clothing, carpet, glass, metal-work, match and fireworks factories, mining, construction, gem polishing, leather tanning, furniture making, seafood canning and other types of food processing, fishing and deep-sea diving.

Children are not often found working in huge factories. It is easier for workers to organize themselves into unions in large workplaces. And where there are unions, child labor is usually prohibited. So when children work in industry, it is usually in homes or sweatshops that supply to larger factories. The work is very labor-intensive, meaning that it requires lots of manual labor and little machinery is involved. These small shops tend to spring up in semi-urban and urban areas where there are many rural people recently forced off their land who need work.

Some of the most exploitative jobs are found in these small industries where local employers are looking for cheap labor in order to make their goods as cheaply as possible. In fact, many of the children working in these firms are bonded laborers (see page 34).

In the charcoal industry in Brazil, whole families of poor migrants are recruited to work in areas far from towns, where there are no schools or health facilities. They gather eucalyptus and pine wood and put it into huge kilns to make charcoal, which is then used to make pig iron for Brazil's huge automobile industry. The families work twelve hours a day gathering and stacking wood, putting it into the kilns and then loading the finished charcoal into sacks. The charcoal dust is thick in the area around the kilns, and workers—especially child workers, who are more vulnerable—have bad breathing problems. They also suffer from poor circulation because of the exposure to high temperatures. Many are malnourished.

Industrial work is one of the most well-known areas of child work, probably because it is one of the most dangerous. The danger is obvious in the case of a glass factory, where children are working with molten glass, or a match factory, where they suffer burns daily. The hazards may be less clear in a carpet or garment factory, where the effects of dust on a child's lungs or of sitting in the same position for hours on end or of poor lighting may be noticeable only after some time. But there are dangers in most of the industrial work children are involved in because of the lack of workplace safety standards.

Many international campaigns focus on children working in the small

industries that produce goods for export to other countries. This is in part because there is a lot of bonded labor in these industries and because the work there is among the most dangerous of all the work that children do. It is also because western consumers are able to exert their influence on the way the goods they buy are produced. Yet these children make up only about 5 percent of all working children.

Boys working in a small factory in Bangladesh.

Ninety percent of the children who work in the match industry in Sivakasi, India, are girls. Many of their parents feel it is pointless educating female children because they need to earn money for their dowries. While 71 percent of the boys in the area go to school, only 23 percent of the girls do. In fact, 60 percent of the girls who work at the match factories do not get paid at all. If they do get a wage, it's only about $1.20 a week.

The match industry has some of the youngest children working outside the home anywhere in the world—66,000 children between the ages of six and eleven—and some of the worst working conditions. Making matches is extremely dangerous. Eighty percent of children interviewed by Pharis Harvey and Lauren Riggin for their book, *Trading Away the Future*, said they had been involved in accidents where they were burnt or almost burnt. They are exposed to poisonous chemicals. They suffer from respiratory illnesses, including tuberculosis, as well as exhaustion, malnutrition and skin diseases. Many reported sexual abuse by factory supervisors. It is no surprise that many of the girls use drugs, and there is a high incidence of suicide at the factories. The fact that most of the workers are girls—and that girls' work is considered less important in the traditional male-dominated society in India—in part explains why the industry gets away with subjecting workers to such bad conditions.

The World's Working Children

Nirmala

Nirmala, Age 10, Nepal, Carpet Weaver

Nirmala Burda Thuki is ten years old. When she was eight, her father took her to work as a weaver in a carpet factory near Kathmandu, the capital of Nepal. Her family needed the money, she says.

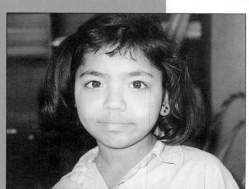

Nepali children like Nirmala work in "factories" the size of a school classroom. A typical factory holds eighteen enormous weaving looms. Five children work at each loom, tying knots in carpets. They start early in the morning, around six, and work until late at night, up to sixteen hours a day. The lighting is usually poor. There are no windows and the ventilation is bad. There are no washrooms. Most of the children eat only twice a day—around eleven in the morning and seven at night—and they are always hungry. They sleep in the factory, many to a room. This "room and board" is all many of the child workers receive for their work.

Weaving is painful work, even after you've learned how to do it. The children say that their hands get numb moving their fingers between the stiff threads of the loom. The cramped quarters, long hours, poor nutrition, lack of air and wool dust cause sore backs and respiratory illnesses like coughs and, in some cases, tuberculosis.

In Nepal, there are many children like Nirmala. Most are brought from poor communities outside the city by a labor contractor or tekhadar. Some are brought by their own parents. The payment for the child's work is usually handed over to the parent or the tekhadar. In many instances, children are paying off a loan their parents have already received. In other words, they are bonded laborers.

Carpets are very important to Nepal's economy. In 1993 they made up 60 percent of its export income. There was a huge decrease in carpet exports in 1994, in part because of overproduction and poorer-quality carpets. However, the decline was also due to international pressure put on the country because of its use of child labor. A short piece on German television had an enormous impact when it stated that children helped produce 90 percent of Nepal's carpets.

In 1994, thousands of children in Nepal were evicted from factories because of this negative publicity and the resulting government crackdown on child labor. (The legal working age in Nepal is fourteen, but the law has not been enforced.) This gave non-governmental organizations (NGOs) an opportunity to help child workers like Nirmala.

Nirmala had been working as a weaver for two years when she was invited to attend a school for displaced carpet children. The school provides its ninety-five students with food and shelter, health care, schooling

Listen to Us

Nirmala at the School for Displaced Carpet Children, Nepal.

Non-Governmental Organizations (NGOs)

NGOs are different from individual government bodies (e.g., the Swedish International Development Agency, SIDA) or United Nations bodies (e.g., UNICEF) that are formed by UN member countries. NGOs are also non-profit, unlike private organizations. They usually develop in response to a need in the community and work in an area where the government is not doing its job or feels it has no place. NGOs may start small and grow, like Greenpeace. Or an NGO may confine itself to a particular community and stay small.

Some examples of NGOs that deal with the issue of child labor:
• Anti-Slavery International (based in London, England)
• Bonded Labor Liberation Front (Lahore, Pakistan)
• Butterflies (New Delhi, India)
• Child Labor Coalition (Washington, D.C.)
• Child Workers in Nepal Concerned Centre (Kathmandu, Nepal)
• Free the Children (Toronto, Canada)
• Save the Children (London, England)
• South Asian Committee on Child Servitude (New Delhi, India)
• Street Kids International (Toronto, Canada)

and job training. The children also have several hours of free time a day.

For Nirmala, like most of the other children, the chance to study is the best thing about the school. The "good food" comes next on the students' list. Nirmala also says she loves to play badminton and soccer, both of which she learned at the school.

Teachers point out that the children's experience as workers has made them extremely hard-working at their studies. As one said, "They're used to sitting at looms from 6 A.M. to 10 P.M. daily, seven days a week. I've never seen kids so disciplined in my life."

Nirmala will study at the school for two years and then, it is hoped, be able to find a better job. Ideally she will be able to keep going to school. She will need much more education and the money to pay for it in order to realize her dream, which is to be a doctor.

Nirmala is one of the lucky ones. Thousands of other children were also displaced from their carpet-weaving jobs. Some do domestic chores during the day and weave secretly at night in their original factories. (One local organization says that half of the country's carpet workers are still under fourteen.) Others have moved to smaller factories where they are less likely to be noticed by police. Still others have moved to industries that employ large numbers of children—they make bricks, serve food in small tea shops, or have become sex workers.

Street kids in Nepal (above) and Peru (right).

Working on the Street

There are tens of millions of street children in the world's cities, in both developing and industrialized countries. Only about one in ten of the children we see working on the street—hawking jewelry, selling newspapers, shining shoes, guarding cars, scavenging for food, paper or plastic (ragpicking), begging, sometimes stealing—actually live there, however. Most of them return to their families at night. Although their families are in most cases extremely poor, they at least offer affection and some protection.

Some street children live on the street full time. They may have left home because their parents were too poor to care for them. Or they were abused and ran away. Others were forced to leave their rural homes or were separated from their families because of war. This was true of 90 percent of the Liberian children UNICEF found living or working on the street in 1991.

Whether they live there full time or not, street children are not being supervised by adults at home or at school. They spend their time in the busy urban area of offices, stores and restaurants, which is thought to be the domain of adults. It is not the place where a child alone is supposed to be found.

There is no typical street kid, because conditions are different in every country. But all street children do spend most of their time on the street, trying to eke out some sort of a living. It is not an easy or a safe place to be. As Margaret, a young girl interviewed by UNICEF in Rio de Janeiro, Brazil, notes, life on the street is best described as violent:

> Being hungry is violent, sleeping on the cold ground, prejudice from society—there are many ways a child can be subjected to violence. On the street I would approach a person to sell sweets and they would spit at me. Not being able to fight back on the street, that is violence. The fact that I am black made it worse.

Some street kids join gangs for support and protection. They are often trained to be pickpockets or to steal in other ways. Many are introduced to drugs. Glue-sniffing is relatively cheap and it helps mask

In Brazil, the government, NGOs and UNICEF are trying to help street kids by setting minimum prices for a shoeshine, for example.

The World's Working Children

Many street children live in shanty towns that edge the cities, in shacks made of building scraps or leftover cardboard. There is often no running water, no electricity, no garbage disposal, no schools, and nowhere to grow food. This one is in Bangkok, Thailand.

their hunger and fear. It also makes them less aware of other dangers—like a fast car moving past them on the street—which means they are more vulnerable than ever.

There are many more boys on the street than girls—or at least boys are more visible on the street. Girls who have left home are more likely to be working as domestic servants or as sex workers. Some girls pretend they are boys so they will be less vulnerable to sexual threat.

Cities are getting bigger as rural people, no longer able to make a living off their land, move to the urban areas. In the last thirty years, 70 percent of the population of Latin America has left the rural areas to go to the cities. There are an estimated 8 million street children in the cities of Latin America, mainly in Brazil, Colombia and Mexico. There are also large numbers of street children in South Asian and African cities. The numbers of street children in the former Soviet Union are increasing with the collapse of state-funded social-welfare programs. Russia alone has an estimated 500,000 orphaned and abandoned children. More children are living on the street in Europe and North America, too, as huge layoffs leave many families without jobs, and social-welfare programs are cut back.

Street children face many hazards: malnutrition; illness; physical injury from hostile adults, including police, or being hit by vehicles; arrest for petty crimes; drug addiction and sexually transmitted infections (STIs), including AIDS. In Brazil, where their numbers have soared dramatically in the last few years, they also face execution by unofficial death squads. In June 1993, a group of off-duty policemen shot eight children who were sleeping on the steps of the huge Candeleria Church in Rio de Janeiro. The kids had apparently thrown stones at a police car the day before. In 1994, 1,274 children died violent deaths in the state of Rio de Janeiro, which includes the city; 574 of these were shot to death. Human rights worker Jan Daniels told Toronto *Star* reporter Linda Diebel in 1996:

> These are poor kids, mostly black, but people here do not think of them as children. They see them as criminals in the bodies of children.... Face it, people are scared to death of these kids....When you have 30,000 street kids in your city and the government doesn't do anything, you become passive about what you'll accept. That includes allowing police to murder kids.... I don't say Brazilians don't care as individuals—they do—but ... people just don't know how to fight back.

United Nations organizations and NGOs run hundreds of programs worldwide to help street children. Some offer food and health care for the street kids. A few provide full-time room and board and schooling. More recently, programs have begun to focus on providing better services to the urban slums where many street children live, as well as finding ways to help their families make money.

A girl on the outskirts of Cairo, Egypt, where there are 60,000 street children.

Street Kids International (SKI) recognizes that street kids are tough, courageous survivors. Noting that most street kids are already making money, SKI helps them work together more efficiently and safely. As Chris Lowry of SKI says, "In the best of all possible worlds children don't work, but today we need to meet them on the street and meet the working children where they are, in their reality, and help them improve their well-being."

After input from NGOs in Tanzania, Zambia, India and Mexico, SKI developed *The Karate Kid*, an animated video demonstrating the dangers of AIDS, and *Goldtooth*, which tackles substance abuse. The cartoon characters are based on real street children and their daily problems—being lured into sex work and drug abuse, being beaten by police. In *Goldtooth*, the Karate Kid, the smaller children's protector and helpmate, reveals his own tragic back-

ground of drug abuse. When he finishes, he looks at the camera and says, "That's my story. What's yours?" Community workers then discuss the video with the kids who are watching and encourage them to talk about their own lives.

Not only have the two videos made the discussion of taboo subjects like sex and drug abuse a lot easier, they have inspired people working with street kids to see them in a different light. As one community worker noted,

I realize why I get nowhere with my [kids] when I focus only on the negative consequences of drug use. It's like I set aside all that I know about the struggles they have and can't give them credit for trying to take care of themselves in one of the few ways they see available to them.

Left, right and bottom right: Street kids in Canada, Poland and Brazil.

Scenes from *The Karate Kid*.

In Brazil in 1986, 432 street children between the ages of eight and sixteen met for two weeks to discuss their work, education, families and health. The workshop on violence—in particular, police violence—was of greatest interest to these children. Their list of demands at the end of the conference included a law against violent treatment, better schools, free textbooks, better pay for their parents, laws to regulate children's work and their wages, and a union for child workers.

The World's Working Children   51

Sex Work

A million children a year are drawn into the commercial sex trade. Most of them are poor and are between the ages of thirteen and eighteen. Girls make up the majority of child sex workers.

Some children are kidnapped outright and sold like slaves to a pimp or brothel. Some are conned into believing that they are being taken to the city "to get a good job with lots of money," not suspecting the work they will be forced to do. Some are sold into the sex trade by their parents, who see it as the only alternative to the family's poverty. Others have left abusive homes and view prostitution as the easiest way to make a living on the street. Still others have been forced onto the street because they have lost their parents or become separated from them during a war. There are even examples of middle-class children in industrialized countries who have sex with older men so they can buy expensive clothes and accessories.

The child sex industry is worth billions of dollars worldwide. And it's growing as a result of globalization, the growing inequality between rich and poor, increased consumerism, war and the widespread migration of people from village to city and from country to country. The child sex industry has also been affected by some customers' mistaken belief that they are less likely to get AIDS from young sex workers.

Many countries in Asia and South America have huge numbers of child sex workers. More recently, the countries of eastern Europe— Russia, Poland, Romania, Hungary and the Czech Republic—have had an enormous increase in child prostitution. Child sex workers are also clearly evident in the cities of North America and western Europe, where photographs and films of children being sexually exploited are sold in the underground pornography market. They are distributed in magazine and book stores, by mail and over the Internet. The sex trade also goes hand in hand with the drug trade in western countries. In fact, a common method of bringing children into the sex trade is to give young girls (and some boys) drugs. They are then drawn into prostitution as a way of paying for their very expensive drug addiction.

Instead of seeing them as among the most exploited of children, many people think of child sex workers as little adults who have decided to give up their innocence and therefore deserve whatever happens to them. Often it is the child workers who are arrested and treated as criminals, while the exploiters—traffickers, pimps, brothel owners, customers—get away. When the children die of AIDS or are murdered on the street, no one seems to care. What happened to these children's rights?

End Child Prostitution in Asian Tourism
One of the major NGOs dealing with the sexual exploitation of children is End Child Prostitution in Asian Tourism (ECPAT), which began in Thailand but has grown to be a global network that includes forty countries.

Child Sex Workers in Selected Cities and Countries	
Bogota, Colombia	3,000
Brazil	500,000-2,000,000
Calgary, Canada	200
Dominican Republic	25,400
India	400,000-500,000
Netherlands	1,000
Paris, France	5,000 boys / 3,000 girls
Phnom Penh, Cambodia	10,000-15,000
Sri Lanka	20,000
Thailand	800,000
Toronto, Canada	500
United States	100,000-300,000
Vancouver, Canada	200
West Africa	35,000

Child sex workers are cheated of one of life's greatest pleasures—a healthy sexual development. Their sense of themselves and their bodies may become distorted. Not only is sex work often degrading, but it is dangerous for young people whose bodies are still growing. While their clients may think a young person is less likely to have sexually transmitted infections (STIs), in fact children are more vulnerable to infection than adults. This is because in many cases their bodies aren't yet ready for sex. Children are also less able to refuse to have unsafe sex.

Girl sex workers face the possibility of becoming pregnant before their bodies are really ready for childbearing—and the chance that they or their child may die in childbirth.

Many sex workers use drugs or alcohol to dull their feelings so they can do their work. Addiction to drugs or alcohol causes many physical problems in addition to the need to get enough money to support the habit.

Goldtooth dresses the Karate Kid's sister to be a sex worker.

Sex workers in Cambodia.

Organizations working to end the commercial sexual exploitation of children see it as a worldwide problem that must be tackled internationally. There must be better law enforcement to punish those who are profiting from child sex workers. More and more countries are developing laws to penalize citizens who travel to other countries to have sex with children. Research shows, however, that local men are the biggest clients of sex workers around the world. Therefore all men must be made aware that sex with children is a crime that will be punished. And people everywhere must be persuaded to uphold the rights of child sex workers, rather than treat them as children "gone bad," or as victims who have no personalities and no minds of their own. Like all child workers, sex workers are people like ourselves with the same needs and desires.

Former teenaged prostitute Cherry Kingsley says teenaged sex workers in Canada should not be considered victims. Rather they are troubled people who are looking for a way to survive. "For some of us," she said, prostitution "was the first time we got to negotiate what we were going to do."

If sex workers work independently, they often earn more than anyone else in their family. This gives them more status within their families and helps them break out of their traditional feminine roles. One way to counter young women moving into sex work, therefore, is to make sure that girls have an equal place alongside their brothers both in the family and in society.

Christine

Christine, Age 16, Canada, Sex Worker

Christine Andrews was born in Guyana in South America. She was only five when she was sexually abused by her fourteen-year-old step-brother. Her father beat her mother, and Christine was relieved when they left him for good in 1986 and came to Canada.

Christine began working in her new stepfather's clothing store in Toronto's Eaton Centre when she was twelve. If anyone asked, she said she was sixteen. One evening, on the way home from work, her stepfather raped her in his car. Her mother didn't believe her until her stepfather admitted what had happened, and then she blamed Christine for "leading him on."

"I started to act out in a rebellious way, and to skip school," says Christine. Three months later she ran away with a girlfriend and began hanging out with "tough kids, fighting with teachers and with each other." During this time, she says, "I always had good marks and kept up with my schoolwork."

After a fight with another girl, Christine had the first of many encounters with the police. A few months later, she was charged with assault and went to jail for two weeks. She was expelled from school.

Like many young offenders, Christine's time in jail led her to increased criminal activity.

"I met this girl in custody. She introduced me to the street scene." Christine moved in with a friend downtown and was soon dealing crack and cocaine and "weed."

Christine returned home once and got into a fight with her mother, who had found out she had robbed somebody. Her mother called the police. "Eight cops came. They handcuffed me to the door!" At the time, there were three warrants out for her arrest.

Eventually, Christine was made a ward of the court and sent to an assessment home, where her case was evaluated by social workers. "It was hard," says Christine, "but it was there or jail." She started therapy. "They used to take me to a quiet room where I could yell and scream. I was really mad at my mom."

Christine gave a statement to the police, who arrested her stepfather for sexual assault. After a two-year trial, he was sentenced to a year in jail.

Christine was finally returned to her mother's custody. She went home on a Thursday but was gone by Sunday, back downtown. Soon

she was living with Rosa, a prostitute. She needed money, so she began hooking. She was fifteen.

"It was the hardest thing I've ever done. It brought me down—caused me to lose my confidence. I did it for the money. Starting in May, I worked two weeks straight every night. I promised myself I'd be off by the end of June but all the money went to clothes and drugs." Christine was an independent hooker, a "renegade," but she usually worked on a buddy system with another woman for safety reasons. Hooking was degrading work, though, and hard to do.

"I started drinking, getting really high before going out on the street. I did cocaine five or six times. I smoked weed every day. I paid rent and bought food and clothes. I made about $400 a night, sometimes $800, sometimes only $200."

Christine did move back home in June but it was hard not to have all the cash she was used to having. "I was hooked on the freedom of the streets, which even without the drugs, is addictive," she says. At the end of the summer she went to jail for three weeks for car theft.

"I was very lucky," she says, because of her previous record. "And I promised myself I'd never do it again." She got a part-time job at an adolescent resource center as an editor and design person on a youth magazine. She also went back to school and "tried to turn my life around." It's not been easy.

Now Christine is sixteen and in grade ten. She continues to work on the magazine and writes for Young People's Press. Her stories have been picked up by many Canadian newspapers, including the Toronto *Star*.

There are similarities between Christine's story and the stories of child prostitutes in developing countries. There, too, girls may be sexually abused by a relative. Working underage at a service job, like selling clothes or food, or weaving carpets, makes them more likely to be drawn into prostitution, simply because they are working unprotected outside of their homes.

But there are also many differences. Christine lived with her family until she was twelve. She went to school full time, except during her worst times on the street. For the short time she was hooking, she did not have a pimp taking a large portion of her money or abusing her. She knew about the danger of AIDS and refused to have sex without a condom. She and her family had access to a range of social services—to therapy, to foster homes, to programs for troubled adolescents. She was treated with respect and caring, and her writing skills were recognized and given a chance to develop.

Ugandan boy soldiers.

Working in the Military

Where there's a war, there are children fighting, whether it is in Afghanistan, Bosnia, Cambodia, Chechnya, the Democratic Republic of Congo, Northern Ireland, Liberia, Rwanda or Sri Lanka. Throughout history, young men have always been sent to war. But now, with modern light weapons like the automatic rifle, it is much easier to use children. Less training is required and less strength is needed to be a soldier today.

Children under eighteen helped to fight wars in thirty-three countries in 1996. There were 250,000 soldiers under eighteen worldwide in the same year, some of them as young as five. Some children volunteer to work with the national army. Some join armed groups that are fighting against the state (sometimes called guerrillas) because they want to be part of a national liberation struggle. (This was the case of many young people who joined the African National Congress to oppose the apartheid regime in South Africa.) Many more are press-ganged—that is, kidnapped and forced to become soldiers—by either the army or armed groups. Some children join an army because it is the only way to survive. If their families have been killed or they've been separated from them because of the war, they may join an army to get food and protection. (Many El Salvadorean children joined the Marti National Liberation Front, the FMLN, because their parents had been killed by government soldiers.)

Almost all these recruits come from poor families. Even those who "volunteer" do not have a real choice. City street children and children in the rural areas are at particular risk of being press-ganged. It does not usually happen to better-off children. If it does, they usually can be "bought out" of the army by their parents.

Children are useful recruits because they can quickly learn to use automatic weapons. They are easier to dominate than adults and are less likely to try to escape. They may not expect to get paid. Their lack of life experience also means they are often more fearless than adults. As one UN study reported, "when the shelling starts, the children get over-excited and forget to take cover." As a result, commanders often use children as the front line of an attack.

While the majority of child soldiers are boys, girls have also been involved in some conflict zones. In Uganda in 1986, the National Resistance Army had 500 girls in a total of 3,000 children. Girls working with an army are more likely to be used to cook and fetch water than as soldiers. Many are also used sexually by the soldiers. Small boys are often used to carry supplies and as messengers or even as spies.

Some child soldiers get training to prepare themselves for warfare.

Antonio, a boy soldier at a checkpoint in Angola.

Rahulan Sellathurai, fourteen, interviewed by Paul Watson of the Toronto *Star*, was only ten when he joined the Tamil Tiger rebels fighting for independence in Sri Lanka. The Tigers told him he was too young to fight, so they sent him for training first. He did "boot camp" exercises for three months to develop his strength and then took a year of "commando" training. He learned how to lay mines, fire rifles and rocket launchers and set up enemy ambushes. He first went into combat when he was twelve.

Others get no training at all. They are merely handed a gun and told to use it. In some conflict zones, child soldiers are given marijuana or crack or other drugs to help them get over their fear of combat.

The combat soldier faces the chance of being killed anytime, anywhere. Soldiers are liable to be shot, hit by mortar fire or captured by the enemy and tortured and imprisoned. They risk losing an arm or leg or eye from a landmine explosion. (Children are big enough to set off a landmine, but small enough that their vital organs are closer to the point of impact and therefore their injuries are worse than an adult's.)

If they manage to survive, former child soldiers are often traumatized by the violence they have seen. They may experience nightmares, insomnia (inability to go to sleep), headaches and crying. Other children with brutal war experience become so used to violence that they lose

Helping Former Child Soldiers

Organizations that have set up programs for former child soldiers are learning that local traditional healing methods often work best. For example, western psychology believes that talking about painful experiences helps to heal a person suffering from trauma. Local healers, on the other hand, may encourage traumatized people not to talk and treat them instead using traditional ceremonies that "cleanse" them and welcome them back into the community.

any inhibitions about it and continue to commit violent acts.

Like child sex workers, child soldiers are often blamed for their acts. And even though they have been doing an adult's job, it is often not recognized. In Mozambique, at the end of the war, the adult soldiers received two years' pay and job training possibilities. The boy soldiers received two blankets, food and clothing. It is estimated that the Mozambique National Resistance Army (Renamo) had 10,000 child soldiers at the end of the war, most of whom had been press-ganged. Many of them escaped from the camps once the fighting ended. (It was easier to escape at this point, because Renamo did not want government officials and international peacekeepers to know how many child soldiers there were.) Others probably lied about their ages so they would receive the adult compensation. Another 850 were officially reunited with their families.

It is not easy to find a new role for child soldiers. They have been in a powerful position, wielding guns, and they cannot be expected to return easily to their former lives as children. Even if they do manage to return to live with their families, it is clear they should be compensated as well as adult soldiers.

Anti-government boy soldiers in Myanmar (Burma).

Listen to Us

Naftal, Age 18, Mozambique, Soldier

When Naftal was twelve years old, soldiers from the Mozambique National Resistance (Renamo) attacked his village in southern Mozambique on Christmas Eve. They killed seventy people, including his older brother. They kidnapped his mother, his four-year-old brother, Alberto, and Naftal himself.

His mother and Alberto dragged behind at the end of the line of captured villagers and managed to escape. But Naftal was at the front. "I walked for two days and nights carrying a 25-kilo bag of maize," he said. "Three of the elder women in my community collapsed. The soldiers beat them to death with sticks."

When they reached the base, Naftal was given an AK-47 assault rifle. "The soldier just said, 'You shoot like this. The rest you learn as you go along.' I didn't want to kill anyone. But if I didn't shoot, I would have been shot myself."

After two years of military operations, Naftal was shot in the leg by government soldiers. "There was no health worker at the base, so I just tied a cloth to stop the bleeding." The bullet remained in his leg for two years, and he was unable to walk.

"I lost hope of ever returning home," says Naftal. "I felt that because of my leg, I would stay in the base all my life."

Renamo allowed Naftal to go home after the General Peace Accord of 1992. By mid-June 1994, more than 850 children who had been in Renamo military bases were reunited with their families.

Naftal and his brother Alberto.

But even back at home, Naftal was frightened. "I had to sleep with him at night," says his younger brother Castigo.

Naftal explains, "I kept dreaming that soldiers came to my home and were shooting. They were coming to collect me again. I still get the dream, but less often now. And I am no longer afraid to sleep by myself."

When asked how the experience affected him, Naftal replies, "I feel now that the war has passed, we must forgive and forget."

(Adapted from a feature by Ruth Ansah Ayisi, UNICEF Mozambique)

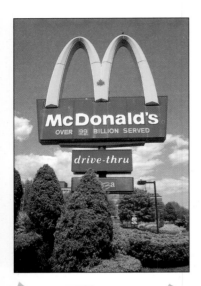

Writer Susan Quattroiocchi calculates that U.S. companies save US$28 billion a year by employing teenagers. Teens do not receive the minimum wage that must be paid to adults, and they receive no benefits. The same businesses profit a second time when the teens spend their earnings to buy their products.

Teens at Work in Industrialized Countries

A surprising 65 percent of teenagers—5.6 million of them—work for wages in the United States. These are not poor children, like most of those at work in the rest of the world. The majority of these American teens are middle-class and go to school. (This figure does not include the estimated 800,000 American child farm workers or the others who work illegally in sewing sweatshops, on the street or selling candy door-to-door.)

Almost a third of these teens work thirty hours a week or more. This means that some of them put in more time at school and work combined than their parents do at their jobs. It is illegal to employ a student for more than twenty hours a week in the U.S., but many teenagers get around the laws by working at more than one place.

In Canada, the percentage of working teenagers is lower than in the U.S., but it is still high in some provinces, like Ontario, at 55 percent. A 1996 study estimated 63 to 77 percent of sixteen-year-olds in the United Kingdom had had a job. A 1986 survey of European teenagers who both work and go to school shows much lower rates, but current rates are probably higher: Belgium, 5 percent; France, 3 percent; Germany, 8 percent; Italy, 4 percent; the Netherlands, 36 percent. In Japan, it is estimated that only 2 percent of the country's school-going teenagers are employed for pay outside their homes. (Recent media reports, however, have stated that one in ten Japanese teenaged girls and some boys have had paid sex with older men. These educated, middle-class teenagers are apparently bored with school and want money to buy designer clothes and other goods.)

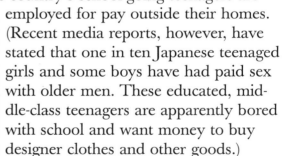

Most of the working teenagers in the U.S. and Canada live at home and do not need to pay for their room and board. A 1988 study of students in Ontario found that only 15 percent were working to help support the family or themselves or to save for university. The other 85 percent stated that their chief reason for working was to get spending money. Paying for their own clothes and entertainment clearly takes some pressure off their parents to provide for them and contributes to the family income. But if their families do not really need the money, why are these teens working? And what effect does it have on their schooling?

With the transformation of society into a huge market, the pressure is on every family member, including well-off teens, to have their own income. Status has become more dependent on one's ability to buy goods than on almost anything else. The situation is more striking in North America than in Europe and Japan, where more importance is placed on educational achievement. There is more competition for fewer spaces in school, the school curriculums are more difficult, the school day is longer and there is more homework in these countries than in the U.S. or Canada. In fact, in Japan, most schools do not allow students to work.

As companies in North America increase their use of technology and rely more on cheaper labor in other countries, thousands of workers have lost their jobs. There are fewer and fewer jobs for students once they finish high school or even university. This makes a part-time job even more appealing. Students think that the more experience they have, the better prepared they will be to find work once they finish school.

North American teens work mainly in the service sector—in the fast-food industry and restaurants, department stores, hotels and motels, and grocery stores. They are hired chiefly because they are cheaper labor than adults, but their employers also know customers like to see young and appealing workers. Teen workers attract teen customers. As an ex-Burger King manager in Canada told Ester Reiter, author of *Making Fast Food*:

They want a certain kind of kid in there. Not the kid that everyone looks down on, that they make fun of. They want the captain of the football team working. Working at Burger King has to be the thing to do.

But the job is anything but glamorous. As Reiter shows, at Burger King workers are trained to do every job so that they can replace each other easily. They are told exactly how much ketchup goes on each hamburger, how many times the fries basket must be shaken, how to greet customers—even how to smile. They have short shifts so they do not need to be paid for breaks. They have no control over their hours and scheduling is unpredictable, making it hard to plan time for school-work and social life. Parents sometimes encourage teens to work so they

Fair Wages, Better Conditions

The National Consumers League in the U.S. has fought for fair wages and tougher enforcement of child labor laws since 1899. It makes the following recommendations for changes in the laws regulating the work of children and teenagers in the U.S.:

• Give migrant and seasonal farm-worker children the same minimum age requirement, the same hours restrictions and the same work-permit requirements as non-agricultural workers.
• Restrict working hours during the school year:
—ages 14-15: a maximum of fifteen hours per week and three hours a day; no work between 7 P.M. and 7 A.M.
—ages 16-17: a maximum of twenty hours a week and four hours a day; no work past 10 P.M. on the day before a school day.
• Require work permits for all those under the age of eighteen. (This will make it harder to hire children illegally.)
• Develop a program to teach children about their rights as workers (salary, working conditions, health and safety on the job).
• Update the list of machines and occupations prohibited for workers under eighteen.
• Enforce existing labor laws that prohibit children's work and enact stiff penalties for violators.

Many teenagers in industrialized countries work in order to buy consumer goods. But why are the goods that we consider necessary so different from the ones that people in developing countries "need"?

We live in a world where making money appears to be the highest goal, and convincing us to buy their products through advertising is the way for big companies to achieve that goal. As a result, we are brought up to be consumers. We are encouraged to use the things we buy—designer clothes, computer accessories, cars—to let others know who we are.

Here are the main characteristics of a consumer society:

• There is a free choice of goods, but the goods are all very similar. For example, there is little difference between two lines of jeans. And too bad if you want to buy a pair of red or checked pants in a year when they are not in style! While we are encouraged to be "independent," we have little real choice.

• Advertising seems to be addressed to us personally. And yet it is actually aimed at whole groups of us, like the "teen" market or the "boomer" market.

• The production process is hidden. We know very little about where and how goods are actually made. Most of us never get a chance to visit a factory to see what conditions are like here or in developing countries.

• Consumerism ignores an understanding of what has come before—of history—or what is going on in other parts of the world.

• The consumer society reinforces traditional notions of women and men. Whether they are pictured in the paid labor force or at home, women are still usually portrayed as inferior to men even in the industrialized world. Most "experts" are white men.

will develop some respect for the working world. Yet this type of work can also make teens feel cynical and powerless.

The positive side of teens working is that their job is the one place where they're not being told what to do by parents or teachers. They are meeting the world on their own terms. As well, their pay gives them a sense of independence and experience in managing money. It also gives them a sense of being employable at a time when young people are being told there will be no work for them when they finish school.

Research shows that teens who work less than fifteen hours a week are likely to get higher marks than both those who work longer hours and those who don't work at all. But there *is* a damaging influence on schoolwork when students work more than twenty hours a week. Many of the middle-class teens who decide to work in the first place are those who are less successful in school. Once they start working long hours, their schoolwork suffers even more. They are also more likely to drop out of school altogether than teens working fewer hours per week. Teachers who know that students are working long hours often allow them to do less homework and do not expect as much from them academically. Studies have also found a relationship between increased working hours and increased delinquency and drug use.

Not only does work give teens less time for school, but they have less time just to hang out, to explore their interests and to think about what they would like to do in the future. While a good work experience has some learning value, being slotted at an early age into a working life in a shop or fast-food restaurant—as part of the cheapest labor pool— does not enhance one's future job prospects much.

Kids and teens everywhere need some time to have fun. These boys in Rankin Inlet in northern Canada are skipping stones.

Sarah

Sarah, Age 20, Canada, Fast-Food Worker

Sarah Inglis started out as a typical fast-food worker. She applied for a job at the local McDonald's in her town of Orangeville, Ontario, when she was just fourteen. She was interviewed on the spot. When asked if she was punctual, Sarah said, "Yeah, sure." She laughs now, admitting that she didn't know what the word meant. She got the job.

Sarah says she wanted to work so "I would have some independence from my parents" and so she could "buy clothes and go to movies and stuff like that." Like most new employees, she was nervous at first. For the first time in her life she had to get a social insurance number and give out personal information about herself. She had to learn new skills—how to take orders and use the cash register. "Nobody ever really taught me how to do the fries, so the manager gave me hell one day," she says. At the beginning she felt a little removed from the "day staff," the adult workers who did full-day shifts. But she made friends with the other teenagers and after a while got used to the ten to twelve hours a week she was working on Saturdays and Sundays.

She was named "employee of the month" when she was fifteen. (For this she got a Ronald McDonald watch and her picture on the restaurant wall.)

Then, "little things started happening." The management started cutting people's shifts so they would not have to give them paid breaks. The adult workers who had been putting in regular eight-hour days were suddenly working three-and-a-half-hour shifts. One of the managers admitted that the reason was "you're more efficient on a three-hour shift, 'cause you start to drag at the end of an eight-hour shift." Workers no longer knew long in advance when their shifts would be. Another manager often humiliated workers by yelling at them in front of the customers. One busy lunch hour, Sarah took a quick breather, leaned against the counter and sighed. The manager saw her and dressed her down for this lapse, and "just made me feel horrible." Another day, a number of the teens were planning a trip to Toronto to go to a prom. They were having difficulty making arrangements for a hotel. The manager said to Sarah, "Why don't you just stand on the street corner and make a few extra bucks?"

Sarah says, "I know it's sexual harassment now, but I didn't know it then. They know that young people don't know their rights." She was humiliated and outraged.

The final straw came when a woman day-shift worker Sarah had become close to was fired for asking a manager to be more sensitive with the workers. Sarah says she was becoming more politically aware at that point in her life. She'd begun paying attention to the newspapers and what was happening in the world. She decided to organize a union in her workplace. She was sixteen.

After attempts with several unions who were unwilling to work with anyone so young, she contacted the Service Employees International Union (SEIU)—and didn't tell them her age. Within a month, she and her friends had signed up 67 of the 102 workers at the restaurant. The union's certification should have been automatic, since they had a majority of workers on their side. But McDonald's heard about the plans to unionize and managed to convince some of those who had signed up to change their minds. McDonald's charged that the organizers had used unfair labor practices and the case was taken to the labor board. "Someone said I held a knife to them!" Sarah exclaims. "And another person said I'd locked her in my car! But the locks on my car didn't even work!"

At the labor board hearing, McDonald's lawyers implied she was an alcoholic and a "dopehead." After four months of deliberation, the company and the union agreed to a vote because there was no end in sight. Sarah explains, "The union never got a chance to call witnesses due to the lengthy trial."

McDonald's gave out "no union" T-shirts and buttons saying "just vote no" and even held a party for the workers. Sarah and her friends were waging a struggle against the multinational that has been unionized in only a few of its thousands of restaurants worldwide. It was uphill all the way. They lost the vote, 77-19.

Sarah is now twenty and enroled in labor studies at McMaster University in Hamilton, Ontario. She works part-time at a designer clothing shop to finance her studies. Sometimes she has had to keep her experience quiet in order to get a job. But she continues to speak to high schools, unions and youth groups. And in December 1995 she traveled to London, England, to testify in favor of David Morris and Helen Steel, who were being sued by McDonald's for distributing a leaflet criticizing McDonald's food and its treatment of its workers. During her day-and-a-half-long testimony, a McDonald's vice-president stared at her for hours on end, sometimes winking, sometimes glaring. McDonald's lawyers insisted she reveal the names of people who had signed union cards in her organizing attempt. She refused and was threatened with contempt of court. They backed off and she was not charged. But it is clear that Sarah Inglis was a big threat to McDonald's four years ago—and she still is.

Job Security, Respect and Dignity

"Wages weren't such a big deal for me," says Sarah. What she was after was "job security, respect and dignity." Some people responded to her unionizing attempt by saying, "You gotta expect to be treated like shit. It's your first job!" But she didn't buy it. "Besides," she says, "they treated the adults who worked the day shift as if they were kids, too." Sarah thinks that schools must teach kids about their human rights, including their rights as workers. As she says, "How important is Greek history when kids don't know their rights on the job?"

While, in its June 1997 judgment, the court found that Steel and Morris had libeled McDonald's, it agreed that their leaflet was true in several respects. The judge granted that McDonald's wages were low, that it exploited children in its advertising and that it was responsible for cruelty to some animals. Both sides claimed victory.

6. Who Says Childhood Is Golden?

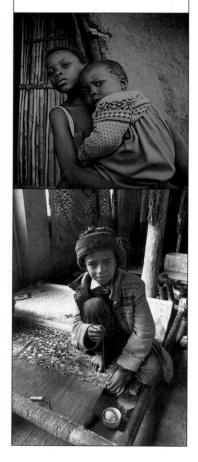

Top: A Mozambican girl holds her baby sister.

Bottom: A boy weaves carpets in a factory in Afghanistan.

Everyone has heard an older person talk about his or her childhood as a magic time when life was sweet and they had no cares. It's a lovely idea, but does it ring true? Are they remembering life as a baby, as a preschooler or as a ten-year-old? Surely they aren't talking about life as a teenager! Or are they? What does childhood mean, anyway?

Think of the difference in the way you and your parents see the world. Then imagine the effects of thousands of years of these "generation gaps." It's easy to see that attitudes toward childhood and child-rearing must have changed a lot over the history of humankind.

Not only are there differences between generations in the same country, but there are differences in customs and attitudes between countries. In some cultures, childhood may last for twenty years. In others, it lasts for three or four.

One thing has been clear at all times and in all places—human infants need to be cared for. They need to be fed, washed, dressed and played with. (If babies don't receive lots of stimulation from their parents and other caregivers, they don't thrive.) Yet in many parts of the world today, by the time they reach three or four years old, little girls, especially, are already beginning to work, usually to care for a younger brother or sister. The same girl is feeding and dressing herself and maybe even helping with chores like weeding a garden, carrying water or firewood or preparing food.

Some historians believe that this was also the case in the Middle Ages in Europe. By the time they were six or seven, children were doing most of the hard physical labor that adults did.

By the seventeenth century, this treatment of children as little adults was beginning to change. As education became more widespread, children spent more time in school and had less time for work. They needed adults to look after them for a longer time. This period of dependency became known as childhood. Children were gradually seen less as helpmates and more as innocents needing protection. They were also seen as needing a longer period of training for a more complex life than their ancestors had lived.

While these changes were true for middle-class and aristocratic children, working-class and peasant children continued to be treated like little adults. And the situation was different for girls than for boys. By the fifteenth century it was common for middle-class and aristocratic boys to go to school. Yet girls from the same classes continued their lives as "little women" until well into the eighteenth or early nineteenth centuries, when they finally began going to school in larger numbers.

Listen to Us

Childhood in Industrialized Countries Today

Over the years the idea of childhood has become the one we're used to, where there is a clear separation between children and adults, at least until children reach puberty. We now make distinctions between baby, child and adolescent, but these terms are recent. Even more recent are terms like toddler, preschooler and pre-adolescent.

In our society, children only very gradually take on the tasks of feeding and dressing themselves. They are unlikely to be responsible for their younger siblings before the age of ten. In fact, their first big responsibility in life is going to school.

In spite of increasing pressure to work for a wage, childhood in industrialized countries is still a time of innocence and leisure. As all teenagers know, this long childhood is not always positive—it can be stifling and boring. Boredom and a lack of independence lead many teens in industrialized countries to rebellion, which takes various forms, from excessive TV watching to drug use or crime.

Childhood in Developing Countries Today

In developing countries, most children, especially girls, have a very short childhood. Only in middle- or upper-class families would you find the focus on a long childhood that you do in industrialized countries, and no one uses terms like toddler or pre-adolescent. In fact, in many developing societies there are no special words at all to describe children between the ages of five and fifteen.

While most countries have laws that require all children to go to school—universal compulsory education—the laws may specify very short periods for minimum attendance at school (e.g., as low as four years). Or they may not be enforced. The children of the rich all go to school, but no one complains if the children of the poor do not. And it is perfectly normal for a poor family to send a boy to school for half a day while a daughter goes out to work in the fields or as a servant in a middle-class family's house.

Children Working—Some Important Dates

1284 Glass makers in Venice prohibit children from working in dangerous branches of glass making.

1524 Martin Luther urges German towns to set up schools. He encourages parents to teach their children to read and write so that they can read the Bible.

1647 Massachusetts (United States) passes a law forcing local authorities to set up compulsory elementary schools.

1723 Swedish royal decree advises parents to teach their children how to read and study the Bible.

1750 -1830 Industrial Revolution takes place. With the introduction of steam engines, factories can be located in areas where plenty of workers, including child workers, are available.

1810 Two children, aged ten and fourteen, working in a textile factory in England, contribute about one-quarter of the family income.

1833 Power looms begin to displace hand weavers in England. With the growth of the factory system, the work speeds up. The English Factory Act prohibits children under thirteen from working in factories. (So at the same time that there is an expansion in factory production, there is also more restriction on child labor.)

1870 -1920 In Britain, the U.S. and Canada, reformers work to prohibit children under fourteen from working and to enforce compulsory education. The developing education system in industrialized countries means children cannot be legally employed while they are in school. So they begin to work at jobs before and after school, on weekends and holidays.

Eighty thousand poor British girls and boys, most under fourteen, are sent to Canada to work as bonded agricultural workers and domestic servants.

1872 Japan makes school compulsory.

1919 The International Labour Organization (ILO) is founded. It adopts its first convention on child labor, preventing children under fourteen from working in industry.

1973 ILO Minimum Age Convention states that no school-age child (under fifteen) can work full time.

1979 The International Year of the Child increases the awareness of children affected by exploitation, abuse, prostitution and life on the streets.

1989 The Convention on the Rights of the Child is adopted. It outlines the rights of every child (anyone under eighteen) to adequate living standards, to social security, to an education.

1995 Iqbal Masih is murdered.

LEWIS HINE

Lewis Hine was a key figure in the campaign against child labor in the United States in the early twentieth century. A New York City school teacher, Hine quit his job in 1908 to work full time as an investigative photographer for the U.S. National Child Labor Committee. He coined the term "photo-story" to describe his work, because not only did he take pictures of children working, he documented as much as he could about them. It wasn't easy to photograph the children, because (like today), many employers were unwilling to let anyone inside their factories. So Hine would pretend he was a fire inspector or an industrial photographer. Once inside, he secretly recorded the children's names, ages, wages and working conditions and whether they had ever been to school or not. He would measure a child's height against the height of his own shirt or jacket buttons without letting on what he was doing.

Hine's photos of children working in canneries, cotton mills, knitting mills, glass and shoe factories, in coal mines, on farms and on the street had a huge impact on the American public and were an important weapon in the struggle against child labor in the early 1900s.

Boys on their lunch break (coal miners?) in West Virginia, 1908.

Listen to Us

Boston "newsies." Some of the boys began selling newspapers on the street when they were only six.

Five-year-old Helen and her stepsisters hulling strawberries in Seaford, Delaware, May 1910. "She started working at 6 A.M. and at 6 P.M. the same day Helen was still hulling strawberries."

7. Children Have Rights, Too

The Right to a Childhood

Most countries have laws governing the use of child labor. Many countries have also accepted the International Labor Organization "conventions" or guidelines, which establish standards for employing children in various occupations. These conventions are not strictly enforceable, but they can be used to put pressure on governments.

Child labor laws vary between countries and even within the same country. Yet the general rule is that the minimum working age should not be lower than the minimum school-leaving age, to make sure that children can finish school before they begin full-time work. For developing countries the minimum working age may be as low as fourteen. It is fifteen or sixteen in most industrialized countries.

Most countries specify a higher minimum age—usually eighteen—for "hazardous" work. This means work "likely to jeopardize the health, safety or morals of young persons." It can include work in industries like match making, glass making or carpet weaving. It could also include sex work or domestic work or farm work. But many countries do not define "hazardous" work so broadly. And there are no restrictions on repetitive work that deprives a child of a chance to learn and develop.

Most countries have laws against slavery and forced labor. India and Pakistan have both adopted legislation against bonded labor. And in most countries it is illegal to have sex with children.

So how do we explain the hundreds of millions of children under the age of fourteen who are working, and the even larger numbers under the age of eighteen who are working in extremely hazardous conditions?

First, not all countries have agreed to follow the ILO conventions. When they do, their laws often apply only to major industries or to those jobs where there is a written contract between employer and employee. That means it does not usually include those very areas where most children work: agricultural work, domestic work and work in the informal labor market (e.g., street selling, ragpicking, home-based factories or cottage industries). The laws also often allow exemptions for "apprenticeships" or the work done in special schools or "training" institutions or the work of child artists (actors, musicians, models, circus performers).

As well, many countries have a narrow definition of hazardous work. Some think hazardous work involves only heavy weights or moving machinery, as in mining. Many allow children to begin to do "light work" at an age below the minimum working age. For example, in Lebanon, children may do "non-arduous work" starting at the age of

Girl on a street in Nepal.

eight. Many countries allow children to begin light work at age twelve. Often there is no real definition of what light or non-arduous work is, but it could include light agricultural work, domestic service, work in shops or markets and delivery work.

A central problem is poor enforcement of the laws that do exist. Most countries have labor inspectors, but they are few and far between. It is difficult for them to examine the situation in rural areas, in small stores or sweatshops, in people's homes. Sometimes employers are them-

THE ILO

The International Labor Organization (ILO) was set up in 1919 to advance human rights in the workplace, to improve working conditions and to promote employment. Like UNICEF, it is part of the United Nations system and operates mainly in the developing countries. Workers, employers and governments from its 174 member countries together develop ILO policy and design programs and projects.

Child labor was one of the ILO's concerns right from the start. One of its conventions, No. 138, states that "work should not be harm-

ful to the child's health or development, should not interfere with school instruction, should not take place during school hours and should not be for more than specifically prescribed hours of work."

In 1996, the ILO approved a plan for a new convention to eliminate the worst forms of child labor, including child bondage, forced labor, sexual slavery, hazardous working conditions and the use of children in pornography. It is expected to be adopted in 1999.

Ragpickers scour a garbage dump in Nepal.

selves relatively poor and illiterate and really do not know that employing children is against the law. Sometimes parents are unaware of the terrible conditions their children are working in. And sometimes the police or labor inspectors are corrupt, secretly alerting brothel owners, for example, that a police raid is about to take place.

Even when the inspectors and the police do their job and arrest those who violate child labor laws, it is difficult to make the charges stand up in court. The workers or their parents are often illiterate and do not understand how to present complaints. They have no access to lawyers.

The whole system favors the employers, because they have money.

With increased awareness of the problem of children working, however, have come better laws and better enforcement. For example, some countries have recognized the problem of (mainly) men traveling to developing countries for the opportunity to have sex with children. In October 1996, a Dutch court jailed a man for five years for sexually abusing children in the Philippines. This was the Netherlands' first ruling on sex tourism. A week later, a British travel agent was jailed for sixteen years by a court in the Philippines for offering sex with young girls and boys to tourists, another first.

Labor inspectors, police and community workers need to know more about the child labor problem. They also need to learn how to talk to working children. They need to listen to children's stories without harassing them. And the children need to learn how to defend their own interests. If they can learn about their communities, and about the political process, they will be able to put pressure on governments to improve their lives.

The Right to Be Protected from Dangerous Work

Many jobs are dangerous to workers' health or safety. Workers need to have safety procedures on construction sites, for example, so they don't fall from scaffolds or get hit by falling planks. They need protective masks and clothing when working with dangerous chemicals in a factory or in a field. They need good ventilation in garment factories so the fabric dust doesn't get caught in their lungs.

A Peruvian boy shovels stone chips at a quarry outside Lima, the capital.

Everybody needs to be able to work in a healthy and safe environment. Yet children are even more vulnerable to workplace hazards than adults are. Because they are still growing, children cannot lift such heavy weights as adults. If they do, their growing bones may be permanently damaged. Their lung development is also not yet complete, so breathing toxic fumes and chemicals is harder on a child than on an adult. Children are shorter than adults, so are closer to chemicals sprayed on crops and therefore more exposed to them. They adapt more slowly to heat than adults, so are more vulnerable in hot workplaces.

There are few statistics on the effects of work on children's physical and intellectual development, or on their life expectancy. But it is easy to see that long, hard work at an early age shortens a child's life.

The following table shows the workplace hazards that working children are facing daily and some of the particular effects these hazards have on children.

The Effects of Dangerous Work

Working Conditions	Type of Work	Possible Effects on Children
cramped quarters	carpet weaving, clothing industry, agriculture, brick and pottery making	sore backs, repetitive strain injury, often permanent damage to still-growing bones
drug-taking (alcohol, amphetamines, cocaine, crack, heroin, marijuana)	sex work, street work, agriculture, some industry (e.g., amphetamines to "speed up" the work)	addiction, weakness, children more affected by drugs than adults, so danger of overdose, death
environmental exposure	street work, agriculture, deep-sea diving, fishing	sunstroke, pneumonia, malaria, drowning, burst eardrums
exposure to high temperatures	many types of industry (glass making, brassware, ceramics)	heat stress, burns and lacerations, injuries, cataracts (a disease of the eyes)
exposure to landmines	the military, domestic labor (carrying water, fetching wood, farming in war-affected areas)	permanent disability or death
exposure to lead	mining, stonecutting, slate, ceramics and glass industries	high risk of contracting silicosis, a lung disease causing severe cough and shortness of breath
exposure to pesticides	agriculture	various illnesses, increased risk of cancers and birth defects, death
exposure to toxic fumes (glues, paints and solvents)	match and fireworks industries, leather trades, construction, toy making	skin problems, cancer, paralysis (the younger the child, the worse the paralysis), infertility and birth defects
isolation	many types of child labor, especially domestic work	depression, passivity, sleep and eating disorders, fear and anxiety
lifting, carrying or pushing heavy objects	construction, agriculture	sore backs, repetitive strain injury, often permanent damage to still-growing bones
machines made for adults	agriculture, many industries, the military, restaurant work	increased strain on body, high risk of accidents causing disability or death
malnutrition	many types of child labor	fatigue, foggy thinking, listlessness, more vulnerable to disease; in long term kids are shorter, thinner
physical abuse (including torture and murder)	bonded labor, street work, the military, many other types of child labor	physical injury of all types, causing, in some, tendency to abuse others, disability or early death

Listen to Us

Working Conditions	Type of Work	Possible Effects on Children
poor lighting	carpet weaving, clothing industry, glass and ceramics industries	eye strain, eye injuries
poor sanitation facilities (and/or contaminated drinking water)	many types of child labor, especially ragpicking and garbage collecting	communicable diseases (e.g., tetanus, scabies), food poisoning, parasitic infection (e.g., diarrhea) causing disability or early death
poor ventilation (lots of dust or fluff)	carpet weaving, clothing industry, mining	respiratory illness like asthma and tuberculosis, life-long breathing problems, early death
sexual abuse	many types of child labor, especially sex work and domestic work, hotel and restaurant work	emotional trauma, higher risk of contracting HIV and other STIs and TB because bodies are still growing, death from AIDS or too-early pregnancy
sleep deprivation	many types of child labor (street work, bonded work)	affects growth and learning ability because children and teenagers need more sleep than adults
verbal abuse	many types of child labor	insecurity, fatigue, depression, in some diminishes will to survive

The World's Working Children

Above right: Schoolgirls in the village of Boubon, Niger.

Above: An outdoor school-room in Hongpogon, Benin.

The Right to an Education

Almost one-quarter of the world's children between six and eleven in developing countries—more than 140 million children—never go to school. Roughly the same number drop out before they finish their schooling. These children make up the core of child workers worldwide. If all the children who are now working were instead going to school, the child labor picture would be very different.

Universal education is not an easy goal to achieve. Education is considered by many to be a privilege of the rich, not something that is everyone's right. Some very poor countries make education a priority for all children, recognizing that the country's development depends on having educated citizens. Others allow poor children to miss out on schooling altogether.

And, of course, even in places where statistics show that all children go to school, many of those children are also spending long hours at exploitative work. So school on its own is no answer to the problem of child labor.

What can greatly improve the situation of child labor, however, is high-quality primary schooling. Schools in many developing countries are overcrowded and poorly equipped. Teachers are often badly paid. Committed, well-paid teachers, an interesting and useful curriculum, good school buildings and materials, free tuition and books are essential.

In its 1997 State of the World's Children report, UNICEF outlines the following as a must for primary schools:

Teach useful skills. Children must learn about their own rights and about labor rights. They must learn skills that are relevant to their daily lives.

Be flexible. Schools must go where children are and must be able to adapt to their needs. For example, if children need to help their parents at certain times of the year, the school should be set up accordingly.

Get girls into school. This is not easy, because it does not follow some countries' traditions. It helps to have more female teachers, to educate the local community about the benefits of education and to provide support to mothers so they can afford to let their daughters go to school.

Raise teachers' status and improve their training. Teachers have low status and are paid poorly in many developing countries. Good wages will attract well-educated, dedicated teachers.

Make primary schooling free. Poor families cannot afford to pay school fees or buy books and materials.

Left: Chinese girls in a village school in Yunnan province.

Right: A UNICEF water project in Cambodia.

UNICEF

The United Nations Children's Fund (UNICEF), is a part of the United Nations system, and celebrated its fiftieth year of operation in 1996. It was set up to improve the situation of the world's children and to protect their rights. It operates in 144 developing countries. Working with governments and NGOs, it supplies funds and expertise to programs that provide clean water and sanitation facilities, health care (especially immunization against communicable diseases like measles), basic education (with a special focus on helping girls go to school) and help to "children in especially difficult circumstances," such as child workers, street children, children abandoned, orphaned or traumatized during a war, and children who have been sexually exploited. It also works to make people aware of the situation of children worldwide, and publishes the State of the World's Children report once a year. (The 1997 report focuses on child labor.) UNICEF drafted the Convention on the Rights of the Child in 1989 and has worked hard to have it accepted by the world's nations.

THE CONVENTION ON THE RIGHTS OF THE CHILD (CRC)

The CRC is a statement of children's rights—to adequate living standards, to health care, to protection from abuse, to an education. The CRC defines a child as anyone under eighteen. It states that all children should enjoy their rights—the poor and the well-off, girls as well as boys, minorities and the disabled. It clearly states that children have the right to play, to leisure time, and to protection from economic exploitation and hazardous work. It recognizes that child bonded laborers and other child workers, street children, child sex workers and underage soldiers deserve special protection. And it also acknowledges children's right to express their own views and to participate in decisions that affect them. By 1996, the CRC had been approved by 187 countries, more than for any other international agreement.

The World's Working Children

<table>
<tr><td>

8. What Working Children Want

</td><td>

We can never really understand someone else's situation unless we're living it. We can learn as much about the situation as possible and try to imagine ourselves in it, but our understanding will never be complete. That is why it is so important to ask the people themselves—in this case, the working children—how *they* feel, what *they* want. And then it is important to listen to what they say.

Most working children are so busy that they scarcely get a chance to think about what their situation means. By talking to other children like themselves, it is easier to understand their shared circumstances. More and more people who are concerned about child labor are beginning to give working children a chance to talk about what they like and don't like about their work. But the opportunity for child workers to speak out is rare, and when they do, they are seldom listened to.

At the August 1996 World Congress Against Commercial Sexual Exploitation of Children held in Stockholm, Sweden, Paul Knox of the Toronto *Globe and Mail* reported that there were seventeen youth delegates—and more than one thousand adults. The teenagers were only given a chance to speak on the second-to-last day of the conference,

</td></tr>
</table>

when many government representatives had already gone home.

"You who care for us, listen to us," pleaded fourteen-year-old Ruby Acebedo of the Philippines. She demanded that children and youth have a permanent presence in government and United Nations forums so that their experiences and opinions would always be heard. Other youth delegates stressed that help was needed for street children and for children in abusive families or families that do not care for them so these children would not be forced to live on the street. A seventeen-year-old Brazilian, Ines Maria Dias da Silva, encouraged delegates to look at alternatives to traditional family structures, pointing out that mothers must have the same rights as fathers. (The less power a mother has in a family, the less power her daughters will have, and the more likely they will be sent to work instead of to school.)

The teenagers noted that it was not they but the sex exploiters who needed rehabilitation. They wanted healing, not rehabilitation. They also showed amazing tolerance for the adults who exploited them. "Everyone deserves a second chance," said Ivette Perez of New York, when she was asked how to punish people who use child prostitutes.

In Nicaragua, the Movement of Working Children has brought together 1,500 Nicaraguan and Salvadorean children between the ages of nine and sixteen. Most work on the street and in markets. Some are peasant children and work on their parents' land. In a series of workshops led by the children themselves, they discussed how they saw their work and the changes they would like to make in it.

First, they said that they are underpaid simply because they are children. And because they are children, the work they do is not recognized as real work. Even though they contribute to their family's income, they are looked down on by adults. They are seen as "street children" or thieves. They are harassed, insulted, humiliated and often beaten.

The problems are worse for girls who work at home. They complained that they are treated as inferior to their brothers and perform all the household jobs themselves, without any help from the boys in the family. Their jobs have even less status than those of children on the street, and they are usually not paid anything for their work. Girls working at home are often sexually harassed and even raped by family members or by other men when they leave the house to do errands. Many children complain that they work such long hours (between ten and fourteen hours a day) that they have no time to study or to play.

While most of these Central American children were pleased to be able to share their small earnings with their families, they wanted to be able to decide themselves how much to hand over. They complained that parents and other adults took all of their earnings without asking. In addition, they wished to be able to decide themselves whether to work or not.

The children described many problems in their work: the exploitation, the abuse, the lack of respect. But they also found their work very positive in some ways. The children who earned money wanted to help

A girl takes part in a UN forum in Addis Adaba, Ethiopia.

support their families. They also saw their work as a chance to learn things that made them more independent. Many children said they enjoyed the opportunity to meet people, make friends and share in other people's work.

These children did not want child labor to be prohibited. They felt oppressed by adults who were trying to protect them by preventing them from working. Instead they wanted laws that would give them better working conditions and higher wages. The right to work if they wanted. The ability to make their own decisions.

For these Central American children it is not work itself that is bad for them. It is their poverty and the treatment they get from adults that is bad.

In December 1994, 1,100 child workers met for three days in the city of Madras, India. The six- to eleven-year-olds were attending the first National Convention of Child Laborers, organized by the Campaign Against Child Labor, a Bombay-based NGO. The children's main demand was to be freed from work in order to go to school. They also asked for schools that were near their homes, free books and uniforms, an "interesting" education, jobs for their parents, and basics such as food, water, electricity and health facilities.

Recognizing that it would be difficult for them to stop working in the short term, the children stated that in the meantime, they wanted safety on the job and job security, meaning a job they could rely on keeping. They also wanted schools, shelters and health facilities made available to children who were working away from their homes. Daycare centers for their younger brothers and sisters would also help their situation. In addition, they said that employers, police and parents who beat and harassed children should be punished.

When child workers are given a chance to talk, it is clear that their ideas are as good as anyone else's. In fact, they're probably much better.

9. Kids Helping Kids

Just as there is no typical child worker, there is no single way to respond to the situation of children working. Some people call for the complete elimination of child labor, insisting that anything less is unacceptable. Others agree that children should not have to work and are alarmed by the extent of child labor, but say that it may be necessary for some children to work in order to support themselves and their families. A third position argues that it is not necessarily bad for children to work, as long as their wages and working conditions are improved.

It is not easy or even necessary to find the "correct" position. But everyone agrees that it is important, as soon as possible, to eliminate what the ILO calls the "intolerable" side of children working—that is, bonded labor, sexual exploitation and extremely hazardous work. Yet even this attempt to focus on the worst forms of exploitation covers children working in many different situations, under many different conditions. And as we have seen, it is not always easy to define hazardous work.

What is clear is that the struggle to help working children must take

In Bangladesh, an American and a Bangladeshi teenager interview a girl who works breaking open used batteries to recycle the parts.

place on a number of fronts at the same time. We must also be prepared to consider a variety of ways of responding to their needs.

Getting Involved
The first step in getting involved is to learn about the issue. Read books (see page 95.) Talk to people. Get a sense of what *you* think are the key issues. Then you'll be able to convey these ideas to someone else. Talk to people in the groups you belong to and see if they would like to help you do something about it.

You can help make changes for working children on many different levels: within your own school or community, town or city, province or state, at the national level and the international level. If you belong to your school's United Nations group, the Guides or Scouts, a church group or a human rights group, get together and talk about what you can do. If you don't already belong to a group that is interested in child labor, you could set up a branch of an existing one, or you and your friends could start your own. Some of the most active and influential campaigns have been those started by children and teenagers.

A variety of agencies, NGOs, activist groups and trade unions take into account the needs of street children, sex workers and migrant farm workers in North America and Europe. There are also organizations that help domestic workers. If you live in British Columbia, you may want to contact Zindabad, the Canadian Farmworkers' Union, to see how you can help publicize the situation of the farm workers and their children there. If you live in California, you can contact the United Farm Workers of America. Or contact your local UNICEF or Save the Children office to see how you can help child workers in developing countries.

The Consumer As Activist
As consumers, we can help eliminate child labor in industries that make the things we buy. If we demand that our clothes and carpets, toys and sports equipment must be made without child

This boy works at his home with his family making softballs in a village in northern Honduras.

A boycott is a refusal to handle, sell or buy a product because you disagree with the way it was made or the way people are treated in the country where it was made. The international boycott against South African products in order to force the end of the apartheid system in South Africa is an example.

A boycott is not always the best way to encourage change in a particular situation, however. For example, in 1993 the United States threatened to stop importing goods that had been made using child labor. As a result, an estimated 50,000 children in Bangladesh were fired from the garment factories in which they were working. UNICEF discovered that many of them ended up in worse jobs on the street or in construction.

A group should only begin a boycott campaign if human rights groups in the affected country are in full agreement about what the boycott can achieve. Organizing a successful boycott requires a great deal of planning and coordination. Boycotts that have not planned practical alternatives for the children who will be put out of work will likely cause more harm than good.

labor, the store owners and importers will begin to listen. Look what happened in 1995 when people realized the Gap was marketing clothes made by workers under extremely poor working conditions. Together, a huge number of North American labor, women's, student, consumer and religious groups put pressure on the clothing chain. The Gap didn't want people to stop buying its clothing, so it signed an agreement that allows human rights observers to check the conditions at all its factories.

Many campaigns focus on getting rid of child labor in developing countries in industries where children are producing goods for export. Here are some of the international campaigns you could be a part of.

Rugmark

The smiling Rugmark label offers hope that in the future, fewer and fewer children will be forced to work as bonded carpet weavers. The Rugmark label attached to a hand-knotted or hand-woven carpet indicates that no children have been involved in making it.

International groups concerned about bonded child labor in the carpet industry set up the Rugmark Foundation in 1994. Members include hundreds of NGOs in South Asia, Europe and North America, UNICEF, the German Development Agency and the International Confederation of Free Trade Unions. It is financed by these organizations and by a fee paid by carpet manufacturers who want to use the label.

So far, about 150 Indian and Nepalese carpet manufacturers (the biggest have up to two thousand looms) have applied to use the Rugmark label. To qualify, they must agree to produce carpets without child labor, pay adult workers minimum wages that are set by the government, register all their looms with the Rugmark Foundation and allow inspectors into their factories at any time to make sure that no children are working there.

It is hoped that eventually other countries that use child labor in the carpet-making business will also want to participate in Rugmark. They include Pakistan, Egypt, Iran, Morocco and Turkey.

Business people who import Rugmark carpets are asked to increase their price by 2 percent. The surcharge is returned to the Rugmark Foundation to help former child weavers. The funds provide children with an allowance and a daily supply of rice to support them and their families so the children can afford to go to school.

There is still a lot of work to do to make sure that the governments in the carpet-weaving countries provide schools and teachers for these children. It is only with pressure from both inside and outside the countries that education will be made a priority for children from poor families. Continued effort is also needed to ensure that the adults who replace the children in carpet factories have minimum wages and satisfactory working conditions.

Rugmark is the first in a number of potential campaigns for child-free labor. A similar trademark could also be used in the garment, footwear or sports equipment industries.

Free Your Outfits

"Libère tes fringues" ("Free your outfits") is a French campaign launched in November 1995 by twenty-seven unions and consumer associations. Its goal is to educate consumers about the social and economic conditions behind the making of clothing. Its first action was to put pressure on France's three large clothing manufacturers—Redoute, Kookai and C&A. Kookai and C&A have agreed to ask their suppliers for a statement that no child or bonded labor is used in the making of their clothing. Redoute has also demanded that its suppliers follow ILO regulations, which would include no union repression and no racial discrimination.

Foul Ball Campaign

The Foul Ball Campaign was launched in the United States in June 1996 by the Washington-based International Labor Rights Fund. It enlisted kids' help to protest the sale of soccer balls (or footballs, as they are called everywhere in the world except North America) and other sports equipment made by Pakistani and Indian children.

Pakistan makes 80 percent of the world's soccer balls. Thirty-five million balls a year are produced for multinational companies like Nike, Adidas and Reebok. In Pakistan, adults in city factories cut out the thirty-two six-sided pieces needed to make each soccer ball. The pieces are taken to villages outside the city where mainly children, cramped together in dingy sheds, stitch them together. A *Life* magazine article in June 1996 showed a three-year-old Indian girl whose hands were so small, she couldn't even handle a pair of scissors. But she was helping her mother and four sisters stitch soccer balls. Together they earned 75 cents a day.

When American children learned that the soccer balls they played with were made by children often younger than themselves, they reacted. And so did the International Football Federation, known as FIFA. The federation ensures the quality of soccer balls, so why not enforce a code of conduct for the manufacture of the balls? In the summer of 1996, it decided it would allow only balls made with no forced labor, no child labor, limits on the hours of work, fair wages, freedom of association (meaning workers can meet with other workers to discuss their rights) and the right to form unions. It also required a contribution to the former child stitchers' schooling.

At first there was strong opposition to this agreement from some companies, who were worried about losing the advantage they get from suppliers who use cheap child labor. In 1997, the Pakistan sporting goods industry, United Nations organizations, NGOs and international sporting goods associations announced a project to eliminate child labor in Pakistan's soccer ball industry. More than fifty companies, including all the major brands, have promised to purchase soccer balls only from manufacturers who participate. This is the first time that local manufacturers, global brands and children's organizations have worked together to address child labor.

Craig Kielburger, Marilyn Davis and Brendon Hill from Free the Children.

Free the Children

Free the Children was founded in Canada in 1995 by twelve-year-old Craig Kielburger in response to the death of Iqbal Masih, who was also twelve. "The differences in our lives shocked me," Craig explains. He decided to find out more about Iqbal and others like him. When he learned about the millions of children working worldwide, many of them as virtual slaves, Craig felt he had to do something. A forceful and moving speaker, he has won interest in his cause from individuals and governments all over the world.

In 1995, he traveled in India and Pakistan for seven weeks, visiting child workers on the job and even joining a raid to free bonded carpet weavers. He met children making bricks, working in carpet factories, in match and glass factories—hungry, fearful, sometimes tortured, always illiterate.

Members of Free the Children range from eight to eighteen, and chapters have been set up in the U.S., Australia, Chile, Brazil, India, Switzerland and Sweden. They have raised $150,000. The money will be used for two projects in India. One is a live-in education center for freed bonded laborers. The other is a project to set up four schools in rural areas for poor children who might otherwise become bonded laborers. The children will receive a meal a day and a daily supply of grain for their families, which will enable the families to live without their children's income.

Before Free the Children began its work, very few Canadians knew much about child labor. Now, many have some understanding of the issues. Free the Children has also managed another difficult task. It has pressured the Canadian government to take a stand on child labor. Craig's trip to Asia in 1995 coincided with the prime minister's trade mission there. Because Craig was receiving so much publicity, the prime minister was pretty much obliged to meet with him and discuss Free the Children's concerns. Following this meeting, the prime minister agreed the government would take measures against child labor. Free the Children has also convinced the Toronto city council not to buy fireworks produced by children and is working to persuade other cities across Canada to do the same.

"We never even imagined the power we would have to bring about a change," says Craig. "The more people who understand a problem, the sooner a change will come about."

The School for Iqbal Masih Fund

The School for Iqbal Fund was set up by students at Broad Meadows Middle School in Quincy, Massachusetts. They met Iqbal Masih when he came to their school and told them about his life as a bonded laborer. When they heard only a few months later that he had been murdered, they vowed to help continue his struggle. The kids sent out flyers, wrote letters and set up a home page on the Internet called "A Bullet Can't Kill a Dream." By the end of July 1996 they had raised $114,000 for the Iqbal Masih Education Center in Iqbal's home village in Pakistan. It will accommodate two hundred children between the ages of four and twelve—either those who have been bonded child workers or those who risk being sold into bondage.

GOALS TO HELP CHILD WORKERS

- elimination of bonded labor and other modern forms of slavery
- elimination of sexual exploitation of children
- elimination of children in hazardous work
- fair wages and safe working conditions for all workers, adults and children (including those working inside the home, on the family farm or on the street)
- the right of all workers, including child workers, to belong to trade unions and to bargain collectively
- increased awareness of the causes—especially poverty—of child labor
- increased awareness of the exploitation of girls inside the home or on the family farm
- increased awareness of the exploitation of children from low-caste or minority groups
- the opportunity for all children to go to school

SOME WAYS TO ACHIEVE THESE GOALS

- enforcement of existing laws that prohibit child labor
- drafting of new laws that make it illegal for companies to hire children to do hazardous work, and strict penalties for companies that do not comply
- enforcement of universal compulsory education laws to ensure that all children—girls and boys, poor children, children from low castes or minority groups—attend school
- a "social clause" in international trade agreements like the General Agreement on Tariffs and Trade (GATT), which would ensure labor rights, including the rights of children
- incentives (e.g., better trading conditions) to countries that commit themselves to ending exploitation of child labor
- replacement of child workers with adults from the same family so that the family continues to have an income when a child is laid off
- alternative ways of lending money to poor families so they do not have to "sell" a child into bondage or send them to work
- more research into the situation of working children
- public education about the situation of working children

A Bangladeshi and an American journalist talk to children in a poor neighborhood in Dhaka, Bangladesh.

The World's Working Children

Glossary

aristocratic – belonging to the privileged or wealthy upper classes

bonded labor – a system in which people are forced to work to pay off a loan

boycott – a refusal to buy or sell a product in order to put pressure on a company or country to change its practices or way of treating workers

brothel – a house where a number of prostitutes work under the control of the owner, who profits from their sexual exploitation

capitalism – an economic and societal system in which the means of production—land, mines, factories and equipment—is owned by individuals or corporations, rather than by government, for their own profit; most of the people in the world survive by working for these owners (also called the free market system, capitalism is widespread in the world today)

cash crop – a product (e.g., cotton, tea, rice) grown for sale (often for export), not only for family use

caste – a system that assigns people their job and position in society according to their birth

consumer society – the society in a free market or capitalist system, where large companies create the desire for new goods and services by focusing people's attention more on what they want—on consuming—than on what they really need

cottage industry – producing goods at home (e.g., clothing, soccer balls); workers are often employed by a contractor who supplies the finished goods to a large company

developing countries – the majority of countries in Central and South America, Africa and Asia where, until recently, most people have lived in the countryside and survived by producing their own food rather than working for wages in a shop, factory or office

domestic labor – the daily work in the home, including cooking, cleaning and child care

dowry – the money or goods that a bride's family pays the groom's family at the time of marriage

exploitation – profiting through the use of someone else's labor

globalization – the process of global integration that takes place as big corporations search for new markets and cheaper labor all over the world

indigenous people – people native to an area (e.g., the native people of North America, the aboriginals of Australia)

Industrial Revolution – the rapid changes associated with the rise of capitalism, the use of machinery on a large scale and the factory system of production that began in England in 1750

industrialized countries – the countries or "developed market economies," which include Europe, Canada, the United States, Japan, Australia and New Zealand

Latin America – the areas in Central and South America that were colonized by Spain and Portugal

middle class – people who do not have inherited wealth or power and must usually work to make their living; they are better off in most cases than working-class people because they have had better access to education and can earn higher salaries

migrant workers – workers who are unable to support themselves and their families near their homes, so must go elsewhere to find work

multinationals – large companies that operate in two or more countries (e.g., IBM, Toyota)

NGO – non-governmental organization; NGOs are non-profit and usually develop in response to a need in the community (e.g., Save the Children)

oppression – controlling people by force or the threat of force; abuse or unjust treatment

peasants – poor farmers in the developing world, who survive by working for big landholders and/or by growing their own food

pimp – a person who offers the sexual services of a prostitute; a sexual exploiter

prostitution – offering sex in exchange for money

ragpicking – sifting through garbage for bits of plastic, paper or metal that can then be sold

sexual exploitation – being forced to offer sexual services in exchange for money (this term better describes the exploitative nature of sex work than does prostitution)

slavery – the condition of being someone else's property, to be bought and sold as the owner pleases

social welfare – a system of social security, which may provide health insurance, unemployment insurance, financial and other assistance (e.g., low-cost housing and child care) to poor people

sweatshop – a small factory (e.g., clothing) run under a subcontracting system, which allows a big company to dodge the legal wages, hours and working conditions a large manufacturer would have to provide

trade unions – workers in a particular trade or field of work form unions in order to deal with their employer as a group (collectively)

universal compulsory education – a government requirement that all children go to school

Acknowledgments and Sources

Many people gave me advice and support in writing this book. First, my thanks to Patsy Aldana, whose idea it was and who wouldn't let me talk her out of it. My partner, Greg Keast, was consistently encouraging and kept me in good humor, and our son, Carl, reminded me how joyful childhood can be. Meg Luxton read every chapter as it emerged, providing inspiration and invaluable feedback. Larry Lyons helped me think through my argument, and my brother, Peter Springer, charmed me with his comments.

I'm indebted to Christine Andrews, Sarah Inglis and Nirmala Burda Thuki, who talked to me about their experiences. I heard Craig Kielburger, Amanda Loos, Amy Papile and Susana Vasquez speak at the "Children at Work: Exploitation Escalates" conference in Washington in September 1996.

Wenona Giles and Moira Hutchinson gave me important feedback on the manuscript. And thanks to Darlene Adkins, Gerry Barr, Paul Fauvet, John Frederick, Maureen Hynes, Chris Lowry, Judith Marshall, Lynn Murray, Ram Prasad Neupane, Purnima Rao, David Rapaport, Ester Reiter, Brenda Roman, Jeff Speed, Rosalyn Train and Howard Wilson for their help.

Many people at UNICEF helped me out: Ruth Ansah Ayisi, Mark Connolly, Brendan Doyle, Madeline Eisner, George Fearon, Shyam Giri, Ken Gray, Stephen Lewis, Patricia Lone, Dan O'Dell, Gerry Pinto, Judita Reichenberg, Rupert Talbot and Ellen Tolmie.

Thanks to the Ontario Arts Council for its assistance through the Writers Reserve Program and to the Steelworkers Humanity Fund for its support to attend the Child Labor Coalition conference.

The staff at Groundwood Books were amazingly competent and friendly. Designer Michael Solomon was inspired as well as gracious under pressure. I was honored to have writer Shelley Tanaka as my editor. Thanks, Shelley, for showing me the ropes.

Finally, I want to thank my parents, Peg and John Springer, for their love and their unwavering support.

Many books and articles were consulted during the course of researching this book, but the following were especially useful. Those marked with an asterisk (*) are of particular interest to young readers:

Bequele, A. and W. Myers, *First Things First in Child Labour: Eliminating Work Detrimental to Children*. Geneva: UNICEF and ILO, 1995.

Black, Maggie. *In the Twilight Zone: Child Workers in the Hotel, Tourism and Catering Industry*. ILO, 1995.

Challis, James and David Elliman. *Child Workers Today*. Quartermain House (Anti-Slavery Society), 1979.

Cheng, Maisy. "Issues Related to Student Part-time Work: What Did Research Find in the Toronto Situation and Other Contexts?" No. 215. Toronto Board of Education, October 1995.

Development and Change, Special Issue on Child Labour. 13:4, 1982.

* Ennew, Judith. *Exploitation of Children*. Hove, East Sussex: Wayland, 1996.

Ennew, Judith. *The Sexual Exploitation of Children*. Cambridge: Polity Press, 1986.

* Freedman, Russell. *Kids At Work: Lewis Hine and the Crusade Against Child Labor*. New York: Clarion, 1994.

Friedman, Robert I. "India's Shame," *The Nation*, 8 April 1996.

Fyfe, Alec. *Child Labour*. Cambridge: Polity Press, 1989.

Harvey, Pharis J. and Lauren Riggin. *Trading Away the Future: Child Labor in India's Export Industries*. Washington, D.C.: International Labor Rights Education and Research Fund, 1994.

Human Rights Watch Children's Rights Project. *The Small Hands of Slavery: Bonded Child Labor in India*. New York: Human Rights Watch, 1996.

ILO. Child Labour: *Targeting the Intolerable*. Geneva: ILO, 1996.

Lavalette, Michael. *Child Employment in the Capitalist Labour Market*. Aldershot: Avebury, 1994.

Lee-Wright, Peter. *Child Slaves*. London: Earthscan, 1990.

Liebel, Manfred. "What Do Working Children Want?" *Close-Up*, February-March 1996.

Machel, Graca. *Impact of Armed Conflict on Children*, Report of the Expert of the Secretary-General. United Nations, 1996.

Marcus, Rachel and Caroline Harper. *Small Hands: Children in the Working World*. London: Save the Children, 1996.

Moran, Kerry. *Displaced Carpet Children: A Case Study of the UCEP/AAFLI Joint Programme*. Kathmandu: UNICEF, 1995.

Myers, William E., ed. *Protecting Working Children*. London and New Jersey: Zed Books (with UNICEF), 1991.

Nieuwenhuys, Olga. *Children's Lifeworlds: Gender, Welfare and Labour in the Developing World*. London and New York: Routledge, 1994.

Reiter, Ester. *Making Fast Food: From the Frying Pan into the Fire*, 2nd ed. Montreal and Kingston: McGill-Queen's University Press, 1996.

Sattaur, Omar. *Child Labour in Nepal*. Kathmandu: Anti-Slavery International and Child Workers in Nepal Concerned Centre, 1993.

Sawyer, Roger. *Children Enslaved*. London and New York: Routledge, 1988.

Schanberg, Sydney. "Six Cents an Hour," *Life*, June 1996.

Silvers, Jonathan. "Child Labor in Pakistan," *Atlantic Monthly*, February 1996.

UNICEF. *State of the World's Children 1997*.

U.S. Department of Labor. *By the Sweat and Toil of Children, Volume II: The Use of Child Labor in U.S. Agricultural Imports and Forced and Bonded Child Labor*. U.S. Department of Labor, 1995.

Weiner, Myron. *The Child and the State in India*. Princeton: Princeton University Press, 1991.

Index

Listen to Us